EX LIBRIS

Becoming Che

Carlos "Calica" Ferrer

Becoming Che
Guevara's Second and Final Trip through Latin America

Translated from the Spanish by Sarah L. Smith

Prologue by Alberto Granado

MAREA
EDITORIAL

Carlos Calica Ferrer
Becoming Che : Guevara's second and final trip through latin
America / Carlos Calica Ferrer ; con prólogo de: Alberto Granado -
1a ed. - Buenos Aires : Marea, 2006.
224 p. ; 24x16 cm. (Marea Overseas; 1)

Traducido por: Sarah Smith

ISBN 987-1307-07-1

1. Relatos de Viajes-Che Guevara. I. Granado, Alberto, prolog. II.
Smith, Sarah, trad.
III. Título
CDD 910.4

Texts and Editing by Constanza Brunet
Collection and Cover Design by Pablo Temes
Page Design by Hugo Pérez
English Translation by Sarah L. Smith.

We are grateful to Liborio Noval for kindly allowing us to use his
photograph of Ernesto "Che" Guevara on the cover.

*In memory
of my friend
Ernesto*

PROLOGUE

Once again I am faced with the difficult task of writing the prologue to a book that focuses on the life of my friend, Ernesto Guevara de la Serna. I say difficult because his multi-faceted endeavors have been so many, so diverse and so extensively covered that without meaning to, I tend to make reference to the figure of Che rather than give due credit to the author of each book.

However, in this case I am presented with the paradox that both the author and I knew Ernesto Guevara de la Serna at moments that were crucial in shaping him into what is today the paradigm of future man. Although it may seem immodest, I use the word "crucial" because I believe it reflects the reality of his life.

Calica (the nickname we always used for Carlos Ferrer Zorrilla) met Ernesto when the Guevara family came to Alta Gracia in search of a suitable climate to counteract the asthma their son suffered. Their friendship began at the tender age of four, as it did among the other siblings in both families. That friendship was only somewhat interrupted by the Guevara family's move to the city of Córdoba so Ernesto could attend Deán Funes National High School. At that time in the lives of both boys, there was a period in which "El Pelao"—as Ernesto was beginning to be known—traveled daily between Alta Gracia and Córdoba by bus. There was another group of students who made the same commute by train, which—by coincidence—I also traveled in at the time as a university student.

A rivalry soon formed between the bus and the train

groups and they decided to settle it in a game of soccer. Since most of the boys traveled by bus, my brother Tomás, leader of the train team, had to seek reinforcements, one of whom was me. That's how I met Calica.

Ten years would pass before we saw each other again. I received a letter from Ernesto announcing that in June of that year (1953), he was setting out en route to Caracas (where I was living at the time) in the company of Calica.

But let us return to the decade of the 30's. At that time, Ernesto was just one more small-town boy; however, the author—without ever straying from the truth—shares details of his life that would play a part in forging the personality of the future Che Guevara.

I consider Chapter 1 to be a marvelous sketch that, in just a few pages, gives an exhaustive description of the place where Ernesto spent his first years and the influence that environment would have on his adult life.

Chapter 2 has the virtue of alerting the reader to the fact that its contents will, while entertaining, offer only what was truly lived by the author and his travel companion. In those paragraphs, a scene written by Don Ernesto Guevara Lynch, reproduced in dozens of biographies, is described, in which he exclaims, "Off goes a soldier of America." For another writer/witness less bound to the truth, this would have been left to stand as a premonition of the future Che; however Calica did not hear the sentence and explains it thus in his story, making his position as truthful witness very clear.

The story of their journey—which I can only describe as extraordinary—begins as of that moment en route to Venezuela, where I was waiting for them. During that journey, they came into contact with the people of Bolivia, Perú and Ecuador, the country where they parted ways, each led to take on the future in his own way.

The story of these slices of life shared by the two, which could have been a monotonous list of names, people, geographic accidents or a simple description of landscapes, is transformed, thanks to the innate story-telling ability of the author and his having lived out the events in flesh and blood, into a vivid tale of the personal evolution experienced by both, but in particular, by Ernesto.

While in Bolivia—always just the same pair of old friends who met in Alta Gracia who grab every opportunity to "paint the town" with friends made along the way or pick up any girls that cross their path—they observe the enormous difficulties faced by the dawning revolution in a Bolivia weighed down by 500 years of exploitation both from within and without. [Such a history] prevents the new and presumably revolutionary leaders from seeing how abusive being sprayed with disinfectant before a meeting with fellow-revolutionaries is for a human being. Ernesto did perceive this, denominating it the "DDT revolution."

Another aspect of their trip that Calica fully conveys is the racial discrimination they witnessed. He makes use of the chapter on Perú to highlight this element, not with catchy phrases, but rather with a raw description of the events.

Also during the stay in Lima, the author, with great human sensitivity, profoundly perceives and recounts the impression Ernesto's behavior on his first visit had left upon the leprosy patients. At the same time, he realizes that his "sidekick" feels dissatisfied with this aimless wandering and that he, Calica, must attend to his own personal goals, all of which makes their separation easier.

I'm only left with the task of congratulating Calica for having shared his personal experiences, thus adding another very important link in the chain of events that reveal more about the intellectual and political development of this man, today a paradigm for all who believe in a more just world to be built by people like him. In other words, children, youth and adults capable of fighting against wrongs and injustice, who can think more in terms of 'we' than 'I'.

Thank you, Calica, for having brought this breath of fresh air and shown us our friend just as he was, is and will always be: A MAN OF FLESH AND BLOOD.

Alberto Granado, La Habana, 18 September 2005

CHAPTER 1

The Proposal

The true homeland of the poet and each and every one of us is childhood and youth because they are free, they are spontaneous. Life, rules and guidelines will then change the circumstances.

—GONZALO ROJAS, Cervantes Prize

"**G**et ready, Calica—we're off within a year."

"Like hell in a year, Chancho. You've still got twelve exams to go."

"I'll pass them."

"Oh, right, you'll pass them—cut the crap."

"Just you wait and see."

Ernesto's proposal was like most things he did: more of a challenge than an invitation. He was fresh from his recent trip with Alberto Granado through Latin America, and like the rest of his friends and family, I couldn't get enough of the stories and anecdotes from that incredible journey. At first we had followed their escapades through their correspondence with the Guevara family, devouring those letters like an adventure novel. Thus Ernesto returned as a hero in our eyes; in admiration we listened to him recount his exploits time and time again. I recall one of our favorite stories: the trip in the Mambo-Tango raft. It was so unstable and difficult to navigate that, even though they had intended to stop in the port of Leticia, Colombia, they weren't even able to get close to shore there and ended up going all the way to Brazil. The raft was loaded with all the gifts—fruit, monkey meat, chickens and other provisions—the San Pablo leper colony interns had showered upon them in appreciation for the dedication and affection both had put into their work there. And they took special care to preserve everything because they knew that provisions would soon start to run low. At one point, a hen fell overboard and Ernesto started to undress intending to go in after it. Alberto very calmly, without putting down the *mate*[1] he was sipping on, said, "Uh, I think you've forgotten about the alligators … " Faced with this hard logic, Ernesto had no choice but to put his clothes back on and grimly watch as his dinner drowned.

The invitation to travel came at just the right time, but I didn't take it seriously at first. Ernesto used his best arguments and charm to talk me into it. He needed a companion to take up his adventures again, because Alberto had remained behind to work as a biochemist in the Cabo Blanco leper colony in La Guaira, Venezuela. The plan was simple: First Ernesto would finish medical school, then we'd start out—by train, thumbing rides, in trucks, on donkeys, whatever was free or nearly free—all the way to Venezuela where we'd meet up with "El Petiso" Granado.

"Look, the oil thing in Venezuela makes for fantastic living; they have a really strong currency, the bolivar, at $3.35 to the dollar. The coins are all pure silver, which basically says it all," Ernesto tried to encourage me. "They've got the best *minas*[2] in the world there," he went on, aiming at what he knew was one of my weak points, "and you can get *laburo*[3] right off, because you don't have to have a professional degree—just a high school diploma is enough to get you any job you want. And the best thing is we can use it as a stepping stone; we save a little, and then we're off to Paris, all three of us, you know?"

The idea of this kind of trip rattled around in my head in the days to come. I was 23 years old and stuck between a rock and a hard place. I had dropped out of

---

1 Tea-like infusion typical in Argentina.
2 Women.
3 Work.

university, my father had died and I couldn't find a job. After three years of medical school in Córdoba, I had realized that the white lab coat wasn't for me; I was more interested in the social and political climate in the Clínicas *barrio*, a real hotbed at that time. My initiation into politics came just after I'd begun university when I was chosen as first-year delegate for the School of Medicine in the University of Córdoba Student Federation in 1948. The federation was divided into two factions: the Reformist Party, of which myself and Granado (who was much older and I barely knew) were members, and another group with communist leanings. I was not a communist, but I was certainly a leftist, a socialist. What we all *did* share was our anti-Peronist, anti-Nazi and the newly emerging anti-imperialist stance. The military police couldn't just trot into Clínicas on horseback whenever they pleased; we covered the streets with marbles and broken broomsticks to keep them out. And an anti-imperialist climate had begun—I signed manifestos repudiating U.S. acts in Hiroshima and Nagasaki after the bombing of those cities. I was clearly drawn to politics, and also—I must confess—the social life in Clínicas was a constant party. My mother finally became fed up, cut me off financially and issued an ultimatum: "Since you've decided not to study, you will come to Buenos Aires and get a job."

It sounded simple, but it wasn't. With no degree and no job experience, a young man in his early twenties didn't have much of a chance of finding a good job. The only real possibility was a government job, but that would have meant affiliating myself with the Peronist party, which I was not about to do. That's how I ended up spending two years in Buenos Aires with hardly any work or school, while my mother juggled what little my father had left us in order for my brothers to continue their studies. I had two things on my mind at that time: horseracing and girls. I'd take on a *changa*, an odd job, whenever I could. That was about the time when Ernesto showed up with his offer that would leave its mark forever. Of course I didn't realize it at the time; I could only fantasize about the easy life, the strong peso, the beautiful women and all the well-paid jobs waiting for me in Venezuela. And I certainly had no problem with Ernesto's ideas about saving our money to continue traveling the world or buying a boat and sailing down the Orinoco River. Alligators, piranhas, indigenous tribes, palm trees, the unexplored... my imagination reeled! I didn't know Granado that well, but I knew he was *macanudo*, a good guy, and that we would get along splendidly. Just based on our enthusiasm, it seemed Ernesto and I agreed on everything, although we would later learn that this was not the case; Ernesto was Ernesto and I was myself. Che was already alive inside Ernesto and pushing him toward a much greater adventure than the one I modestly entertained in my mind. After his trip with Granado, he had noted in his diary:

> The person who wrote these notes died the day he tread on Argentine land again; the one who organized and honed them is no longer, 'I' am not I anymore, or at least not the same inside. This wandering in our 'Americas' has changed me more than I imagined.[4]

The challenge he had proposed was both tempting and unsettling. My friend was pushing me towards an adventure into unknown lands with barely any funds— me, who hadn't traveled anywhere other than to the

---

4 Ernesto Che Guevara, *Diarios de motocicleta. Notas de un viaje por América Latina*, Buenos Aires, Planeta, 2004, p. 52.

One of the first birthdays shared with Ernesto in our house in Alta Gracia. Ernesto, sporting a bandage that covered a recent wallop (bandaids didn't exist in those days); me next to him with my hair slicked back. Our siblings Jorge Ferrer and Celita Guevara (with the white bow behind me) are there with us. Among other guests, there are many who would later become our best friends: the Peñas (Clarita, Susan and Coté); the Muñoz Gonzálezes (Sarita, María Rosa and Queta); the Ayrolos (Barón and Pelado); the Moyano Gacitúas (Teresita and Cornelio); Pipina Hernández and Charo Aguina. And in white, all the ever-present nannies who patiently endured our mischief.

beaches of Punta del Este and Carrasco in Uruguay with my parents on summer vacations! In those days, distances were vast; it was terribly difficult, expensive and burdensome to travel. Travel was only for those with enough money and time to do it. But Ernesto of course had invented a new way of traveling, carrying hardly anything at all, thumbing rides, sleeping wherever and eating whatever he managed to scrape up. Today, after the hippy culture, after the youth revolutions of the 60's and 70's, this may seem very commonplace, but at the time it was an odyssey!

There was no way I could have turned him down. It wasn't the first time Ernesto had challenged me and I had never been cowed by him before. After one of our typical fights in Alta Gracia when we were eleven, he confronted me with his whole gang, of which he was the unquestionable leader.

"Look," he said, "if you want to be in our gang again, you have to do something brave." Not wanting to be left out, of course I accepted the challenge, so they took me to this huge rock about four or five meters square in size with a tunnel underneath.

"If you go all the way through this tunnel, you can be in the gang again," he said. Without thinking twice about it, I headed into the tunnel even though I was terrified that I'd be bitten by a snake or spider, that a frog would crawl up my leg or I'd be crushed in a cave-in. It seemed like an eternity there underground, but I finally made it out the other side and was greeted with congratulations from all. I had reclaimed my title as a friend of Ernesto's.

I've often read that Ernesto demanded of his fellow travelers rigor and stoicism, that they be able to endure heat, cold, hunger and thirst, and that they possess patience when faced with no way out. He would calmly tell you, "Take it easy, we're almost there." That was how it was—you had to meet certain requirements to accompany Ernesto. For this reason, I was brimming with pride to have been chosen to go on that trip. It meant that I had what it took. Even though I enjoyed the "good life"—as I continue to do—I had no problem making temporary sacrifices. He used to tease me about being a *pituco*[5], while he was always happier walking in the mud; he adapted to any circumstances.

Ernesto and I, along with nearly everyone else in Alta Gracia, were brought together thanks to Koch's Bacillus.

---

5 High-society snob.

This often repeated joke (particularly by Carlitos Figueroa, another of our friends) referred to the fact that most of the Argentine upper class suffering from lung disease, whether it be asthma, pneumonia or tuberculosis, ended up in this town in the province of Córdoba. In the 1930's, Alta Gracia was a small, lovely town surrounded by mountains and countryside, blessed with a dry, stable climate that worked miracles that medicine still couldn't offer to people with lung disease back then. In addition, in those days many people considered tuberculosis a shameful affliction, so those who had the means would buy a house in Alta Gracia and endure the matter in a dignified way, claiming to suffer from a more elegant condition that required country rest. The same phenomenon occurred in other towns in Córdoba, but Alta Gracia belonged to the crème de la crème families. Once cured, many had grown to love the town so much that they kept their houses as summer homes or to use in the event of future relapses.

I was born and raised there. My family enjoyed a position of privilege since my father, Carlos Ferrer Moratel, was one of the most important people in this town cum hospital. As a doctor specialized in lung-disease, he never lacked patients. And he attended everyone regardless of economic or social position; he treated the rich, but he also treated the poor without charging them a penny. He met my mother, Dolly, when she came to accompany her cousin who was suffering from tuberculosis.

Many biographers have pointed to the asthma that afflicted Ernesto as of age two as a determining factor in his personality and his life. This certainly was true in the case of our friendship. Ernesto and his family came to Alta Gracia in 1932 when he was four years old and suffering from such severe asthma that a drastic solution was needed. A doctor in Buenos Aires—the prestigious pediatrician Mario O'Donnell, father of psychoanalyst and writer Pacho O'Donnell—recommended a four-month stay in the mountains of Córdoba. Those four months turned into eleven years, a long time in which I had the privilege of living very close to my friend.

I don't remember the day I met Ernesto. It surely must have been at one of the frequent birthday party events our mothers used to drag us to after bathing us, oiling our hair down and ironing and starching us as was typically done in those days. They would have said to Ernesto, "Come on, you're going to meet Dr. Ferrer's son. You two can be friends!" And I, a year younger, was probably told something similar. That was how the social part was handled; you had to be friends with the children of your parents' friends. Our parents met just after the Guevaras' arrival and got along well from the beginning. My father, an asthma specialist, treated Ernesto and, thanks to his good work or to the good climate or to both, he began to improve. This professional relationship was enhanced by a mutual appreciation that grew into friendship. They were both young couples with children the same ages, they both enjoyed a social and economic position that allowed them to take part in the society life offered by the small but distinguished town of Alta Gracia. But more than anything else, they were ideologically compatible. In the insufferably clerical and conservative atmosphere of Córdoba, both the Guevaras and the Ferrers were quite liberal-minded, defending their secularist stance and favoring classic socialism like that of Alfredo Palacios. And both families unconditionally supported the brand new Republican government established in Spain in 1931. The civil war that would soon unfold in that country would divide Alta Gracia's society, just as it would the rest of

Here we are posing for yet another birthday photo in the Peña family's house. Along with Dr. Fernando Peña and his wife are their children Clarita, Susana, Coté and Fernando. The Werner kids also appear (Susana, Marta and Enrique), as well as the Binaschis, Charo Aguina, Roberto Guevara and Carlos Ferrer. I'm in the first row looking off to the side. Ernesto, looking straight on, appears annoyed. Perhaps because he's the only one wearing a wool sweater due to his asthma that summer's day.

Argentina, teeming with Spanish immigrants and their descendents, into Republicans, anti-Fascists and Falangists. The Guevara and Ferrer families were on the same side: that of the Republic.

This political position, even though it contrasted with that of many others in Alta Gracia's upper-class society, did not cause their peers to reject them. The Guevaras, because of their indisputable social status, and the Ferrers, because of my father's professional work, were respected despite their ideological differences. If they were criticized, it was done out of earshot. As far as society was concerned, a heavy-weight family name was no small matter and both Guevara Lynch and De la Serna, Ernesto's mother Celia's maiden name, were well-known and respected by all.

Celia, moreover, was different on her own merit and stood out in every way. I remember her with her string of pearls, smoking black cigarettes with the arrogance of a femme fatale while playing bridge in the Sierras Hotel. She was strikingly beautiful, tall, thin, temperamental and vivacious, always ready to welcome all her children's friends over, always with a book in her lap and she spoke perfect French. She was cultured, elegant and refined and never kept quiet, always had something to say. Celia was not just the "lady of the house", she was quite a character. She had a great sense of humor, always joking, doling out irony and sarcastic comments as well as taking them well. She adored her children, but her favorite was Ernesto, perhaps because he was her first or perhaps because of the asthma that led her to protect and spend more time with him, or maybe it was just that they shared similar personalities and intelligence. Ernesto reciprocated everything; he adored her and always kept her in his thoughts even when he was far away. This was evident just in reading the letters he sent her from the remotest of places. I think he was eternally grateful to her for not having raised him behind glass walls, for treating him like a normal child in spite of the asthma. And she always stood her ground on this issue, even though her husband thought differently—he was much more fearful. Some biographers sustain that Ernesto senior blamed his wife for his son's illness due to an episode when little Ernesto was just two, which his father claims triggered the affliction. They say that Celia took Ernesto for a swim in the Río de la Plata and didn't wrap him properly when they got out, exposing him to a brisk breeze that had blown in. I personally am not aware of Ernesto's father having made this accusation, but I did witness a confrontation over this issue many years later in the Guevara house that summed up the tension between the couple. It was one of the numerous times I had gone to their house for news of Ernesto—who was then already becoming Che, forging his first battles—and found them in an argument. Ernesto senior, perhaps taking advantage of my presence as a potential ally, confronted Celia:

"Look at all this nonsense the boy is up to, we don't know where he is, what he's doing—it's all because of the way you raised him."

"And what would you have preferred? On eggshells? 'Be careful, don't go out, don't do this or that'... No; I decided he would have a life just like any other boy."

I don't think she was wrong—the proof is obvious. Ernesto never felt limited by his asthma; he got what he wanted and achieved all the important things he set out to do in his life. He was always like that, even as a child; never hid behind his asthma to avoid taking on any sport, adventure or game that came up. And whenever he had an asthma attack, he, his family and all his friends took it in stride. We all knew that Ernesto had this disease and that every so often he'd have an episode. We helped him when he needed it, we visited him when he had to stay at home and we were used to seeing him smoke those special cigarettes that were supposed to open his lungs up. (Our friend Enrique Martín said they must have been made out of manure because of the stench!) And we were used to the inhaler, a little device that he had to breathe adrenaline out of when he had an attack. But for us he was always the same Ernesto; we knew that soon he'd be back out riding horses, swimming, playing soccer or golf. His strength, his skill at sports, and later on with the girls, but mostly his intelligence, all combined to make him a natural leader that we all followed. The asthma never got the better of his personality.

Ernesto senior was also an impressive figure—quite tall, thick-lipped and incredibly strong. He came across as always angry, but it was only on the surface, because deep down he was the sensitive type and clearly good-hearted with authentic passion for his children. If anyone did anything to compromise them, he was capable of just about anything. This caged-lion demeanor came in part from the sacrifice of having to live in a place like Alta Gracia with no professional horizons. He would have had much better work opportunities in Buenos Aires with all his family and social connections. Nevertheless, his love for his son and the desperate need to see him get better were stronger; come hell or high water, the Guevaras stayed in Alta Gracia. It was clearly a sacrifice for them. In those days, distance was a nearly insurmountable barrier. Today the 750 kilometers separating Alta Gracia from Buenos Aires may seem like nothing, but back then communications and transportation were precarious at best. Most of the roads were still unpaved and living there meant being practically cut off from what was going on in Buenos Aires. He therefore had to look for work in Alta Gracia where, while it may have been a pretty place, there was no industry. The small town was nearly completely at the service of treating tuberculosis, and then there was the incipient tourist industry. Other than that, there was not much else. For a couple of years, he worked on the remodeling of the Hotel Sierras golf course. But the rest of the time he weathered the storms by leasing some mate-leaf fields in Misiones province inherited from Celia's family. During the years they spent in Alta Gracia, the Guevara family never lacked anything, but they never had much left over either. They lived on quite a short string and were at the mercy of the erratic earnings they brought in depending on the year. This caused them to move often, always to rented houses. And sometimes they fell behind in paying their housekeeper's wages or the rent, but as soon as the long-awaited envelope arrived in the mail, they always made immediate amends. Rosarito, their housekeeper/cook/nanny/sometimes "mother" to Ernesto often told me this, always adding that Ernesto senior's generosity made her forgive him the lapses in pay. Whenever the money finally arrived, Guevara paid her what was owed with an extra month's salary as a gift. He even took in stride the nickname he'd been given, "Urquiza, the Caseros terror[6]", for his tardiness in paying the rent. And he laughed himself silly one afternoon recalling the time when this little guy, Beto Losada, the nephew of the Guevaras' landlord, came around to collect the rent. They were then living in the famous Villa Nydia, which they rented at several different times and was later turned into a museum honoring the memory of Che. Mr. Guevara greeted the young man genially, "Hi, Beto, how's it going?"

"Just fine, Don Ernesto…"

"You look like a guy who's come to collect the rent."

"And you, sir, look like someone who's not going to pay it," retorted Losada, who was quick with his tongue and already well-versed in the difficult task of collecting rent payments.

I personally was a party to Mr. Guevara's matter-of-fact attitude toward money once. I had been invited to go to with my friend Ernesto and his family to spend a few days in Buenos Aires. At one point, Mr. Guevara

---

6 Play on the word "caseros" which is the name of an important battle (fought by General Urquiza), but can also mean "landlords".

discovered that he hadn't brought enough cash for the trip and, without thinking twice, asked me to lend him the few pesos my parents had given me for spending money. Noblesse oblige, that money was dutifully reimbursed to me the following day "with interest". There's also one other event that stands out in my memory from that trip that really captures his character. We were on the train to Buenos Aires and Celia was carrying Ernesto's younger brother, Juan Martín, who was a baby at the time. After lunch, she asked the waiter if he could warm up a bottle for the baby. The waiter rudely replied that 'no, he couldn't—he was working'. He had no idea who he was dealing with. Guevara jumped up, grabbed the waiter by his lapels and started shaking him like a feather pillow. He yelled, "Who do you think you are, damn it, to talk to my wife like that!" They had to pull him off of the guy because he was about to kill him. We kids just watched calmly; we knew no one could outdo him in a hand-to-hand fight because he was phenomenally strong. And despite his easygoing way with everyone, he never forgot he was a Guevara Lynch.

The relationship between the Ferrer and Guevara families grew closer over the years thanks to the friendship among their children. On our side, I was followed by my brother Jorge, who we all called El Gordo and then the youngest, Horacio (Chacho to his close friends and family), who are both doctors today. In the Guevara family, Ernesto was the eldest, followed by Celia, Roberto, Ana María and Juan Martín, who came along much later—nearly a grandchild—who we all called Patatín. Ernesto and I were practically attached at the hip; my brother Jorge, closer in age to Roberto, became his friend; and Chacho and Ana María were about the same age.

The Peñas were another family who were quite close

Another birthday photo on the stairs in our house, where I'd later
be photographed with Camilo, Ernesto's son. Here, I'm the one who
appears annoyed, maybe because I was dressed the same—as was
customary then—as my younger brother, Jorge; we're both in dark shirts.
Ernesto (above to the right) was with his siblings Celita (the one looking
down) and Ana María (the baby of the family) in the front row.
Other guests included Martita and Pipina Hernández, the Ayrolo brothers
and the Moyano Gacitúas.

to the Guevaras and influenced their decision to stay.
Fernando Peña, a judge in the city of Córdoba, was also
liberal-minded and progressive in his ideas. They lived
in the Alto, the part of town where the Guevaras always
rented; the children—Clarita, Susana, Fernando and
Coté—also became fast friends with the Guevara kids.

Life in Alta Gracia was very small-town and quiet.
The days turned into weeks, months and years that
passed without many changes. What might have been a

tedious or suffocating environment for an adult for us meant extraordinary freedom. The absence of danger and urgency allowed our parents to adopt an "outdoor" approach to child-rearing from a very early age. Ernesto was born to live this way—except for the times when he had to stay indoors because of his bouts of asthma, he was as free as a bird just like the rest of us, perhaps even more so from periodically being forced to stay inside; maybe this made him cherish freedom even more, the outdoor life, the small challenges offered by the sierras, the creeks. We children were lucky enough to live in an enchanting town where not only could we just show up for lunch or afternoon tea at anyone's house, but were also surrounded by a spectacular landscape that inspired us to feel adventurous in our excursions to the hills, our plunges into the creeks, our improvised soccer matches or battles in the open lots. Our freedom was only barely tainted by the occasional recriminations of some poor neighbor who had suffered one of our *macanas*[7], dragging us by the ear to our houses: "Look, Don Guevara or Don Ferrer, this little brat has just ...!" Then we'd be punished and have to stay inside. The one daily rule we had to abide by was coming home in time for lunch and being sure not to bother the adults' sacred siesta time. At least this was the case in our house, since my father had to return to his office, so lunch couldn't be held up or else he wouldn't have time for his nap. And as told by a Cordoban patriarch, "At siesta time, only the *porteños*[8] and the iguanas come out." But at the Guevara house, mealtime was another story entirely, just like all the other things that they did their own way— very rare in those days when social norms were much

---

7 Naughty tricks.
8 People from the port city of Buenos Aires.

more rigid than they are today. In their house, you could eat up until three o'clock and you could show up without an invitation. I loved going to their house and did so frequently. One summer day, I was playing in the Hotel Sierras pool with a friend I had invited home for lunch when I realized that it was already one o'clock. I was late again, just like so many other days then; my father had threatened me, "The next time you show up late for lunch ... "

So I said to my friend we should go to the Guevaras' to eat. Celia greeted me with a smile like always, the one that made you feel like part of the family, "Hi, Calica, how are you? What's up?"

"Well ... I had invited my friend here to lunch, but it got late on me and if I go home now my dad will kill me. Do you mind if we stay to eat?" She laughed in conspiracy, kindheartedly inviting us in, the party-crasher along with his guest! There was always enough food to go around in their house—if more people came by, they just fried more eggs or potatoes or they sliced the meat a little thinner so there was enough for everyone.

And of course Ernesto also came to my house whenever he wanted, either to play or to share a meal; but it was always more fun at the Guevaras'. There were always lots of people and an undeniably jovial atmosphere. I believe this contradicts the common assumption about their marriage; at that time at least, their home felt like a place full of warmth. Of course they were both very intense in their way of talking—they debated with each other and all their guests. When I first saw this as a child, it really surprised me, but then I got used to it and took their arguments in stride, just like the rest of the family. Besides, this passionate style of speaking was the general tone in their house and part of its charm. In the Guevara household, you could throw the most trivial subject in the world on the table and end up with a fabulous discussion. They celebrated knowledge, diction and eloquence and the most mundane chats would end up escalating into heated debates. When it was over, everyone would take their leave as if nothing had happened, ready to take up the topic at the next get-together. The Guevara children began to take part as they grew older; we, the guests or stragglers, also managed to get a word in whenever we were brave enough. But you couldn't just say anything—you were cut off the minute you uttered anything stupid. I was quite timid, although as an adolescent I did venture to make the occasional comment; however, I usually kept my ideas to myself.

When the conversation ended, I'd pull Ernesto aside and say, "Well, I think such and such ... "

And he'd come back with, "Well, say so if you're so sure."

"But ... I just didn't have the nerve, so I'm telling you," I'd confess.

And the Guevaras' door was open to all of their children's friends, regardless of who they were—it didn't matter if you were rich or poor, if you had an important family name like theirs or not. Ernesto shared this quality—he could rub elbows with the upper crust of Alta Gracia, but he also had friends who could barely read or write from very humble families, the golf course caddies, the children of caretakers who looked after the houses that were empty in the off-season. With them our excursions to the hills were a bit more daring than what we, the "well-to-do" kids, were allowed by our parents. We hiked to remote places such as some nearby quarries. We'd take bread and mate and not come back until nightfall. And if anyone wanted to accept a kindly offer from a passing truck-driver to give us a lift home,

Ernesto always declined, so the rest of us could only go along with him for fear of seeming like sissies. Ernesto was pure curiosity, absolutely attracted to the unknown. He did his best to get involved in everything, to explore new places, to know more. And what he learned, what he had, what he knew, he shared with everyone—he was generous by nature. Celia often complained that, because Ernesto was always giving away his *guardapolvos*[9] to poor schoolmates, she would often find that he didn't have one to wear himself. If he had any money in his pocket—which wasn't often—he immediately treated all his friends to the 15-cent bologna and cheese sandwiches they sold in the shop close to his house. He also taught them how to ride a horse, which at that time was the utmost aspiration of any boy and was beyond reach for kids from poor families. The Lone Ranger was all the rage at the local cinema then. The hero was always a cowboy on his horse, so if you had a horse and a wide-brim hat, you could impress just about anyone. Even the Guevaras only had horses while Ernesto's father worked on the golf-course remodeling. We, on the other hand, thanks to my father's good financial position, always had horses with good saddles for showing off and impressing the girls. This of course caused a good deal of envy, scuffles and insults. When I'd pass by on my horse, Ernesto and his country friends would ambush me from a makeshift trench that they used for playing war games. So I'd then go off and round up other friends who also had horses and we'd counter-attack by running them down on horseback. Ernesto and I would stay angry at each other and go for days without speaking until we finally got over it and went back to being friends like always. The

---

9 Long jacket worn over clothes to school.

friendship between our parents helped to smooth out the clashes between us owed to our strong personalities. Nevertheless, we never came to blows, I think because we respected each other; maybe due in part to dignity and in part to diplomacy, we never let things get out of hand. There was certainly an element of prudence as well, because neither of us liked to lose. And Ernesto, even though he was capable of meeting a train head-on, also knew just how far he could go. He never fought with any of the other good friends with whom he shared different moments of his life either—Alberto Granado, the Figueroa brothers or my brother, Jorge.

Summer was when our small town awoke from its long winter sleep that had only been briefly interrupted by Golf Week and the school winter break. The "good" families arrived along with the good temperatures to take up residence in their summer homes or in the Hotel Sierras. We kids would go to the station to see who was arriving, find friends from previous summers, see a girl we had our eye on, dodging between the trunks and luggage brought by families who came to spend the summer, while the porters went about lifting them onto the horse carts awaiting the visitors. They were full-fledged moves the vacations of these families, spanning the entire period from early December until the day before classes began in March. The Rayo del Sol train, on the Mitre line from Retiro Station in Buenos to Alta Gracia, was very *bacán*[10]—it had sleeping cars, a dining car, all of the best quality. It ran at night and arrived in Alta Gracia in the morning. Ernesto and I made this trip together many times, both with our families as children and alone when we were older. I remember the plate of vegetable consommé followed by two courses and

_____

10 Luxurious.

In Alta Gracia, the Ferrer and Guevara families moved in progressive and intellectual circles which included notable Spaniards in exile during the Spanish Civil War. In the top photo, from right to left: Paco Aguilar (distinguished Spanish musician), the poet Rafael Alberti, the famous composer Manuel de Falla, Juan Aguilar (former Republican official) and, between two people I don't recognize, is my father in profile, Dr. Carlos Ferrer Moratel.

The lower photo also shows my father surrounded by all these celebrities. The house where Manuel de Falla lived in Alta Gracia has since been converted into a museum that houses photos and many other memorabilia of the great composer and a way of life long vanished.

dessert. And then the adults had their glass of whisky. By the time we got to Rosario, the waiters would get fed up with our antics and throw us out of the dining car, "Out of here, you little brats!" And then we'd go to the sleepers and talk until we fell asleep. The next day, we'd wake up in Alta Gracia to celebrate our return home and re-connect with all our friends.

Everything changed in summer—the activities, the games, our schedules and our friends. Something else that changed, even though it weighed upon us because we loved our year-round friends, were the lines drawn between social classes. These were the times when domestic servants were deferential even to children, calling us "Master" Ernesto and "Master" Calica. The summer-time center of life in the town was the Hotel Sierras with its pool, golf course and tennis courts; its orchestra, balconies and drawing rooms; its famous bar, dances and social life. It was what one would call a 5-star hotel today. Built by the English at the time the railways were being laid in Argentina, it was modeled on another British hotel in Calcutta with the same purpose in mind: a comfortable place for relaxation and sports that replicated the luxurious European lifestyle in the underdeveloped places in which they did business. And not just anyone could go there. There was a marked division, an enormous "sieve", whereby only those who met with the hotel manager's approval were allowed in. The manager was a short Italian, Don Roque Celentano, whom we gave not a few gray hairs. The kids who had the green light at the hotel were the Guevaras, the Ferrers, the Figueroas, the Peñas, the Ayrolos, the Achával Cafferatas, the Marcó del Ponts, the Lahittes, the Werners, the Sánchez Chopiteas, the Fauvetys, the Palacios, the Hernández and many others. However, if we got out of line, Celentano would grab us—Ernesto,

Carlitos Figueroa or me—and send us home packing. Then he'd have a talk with our parents, who scolded us or punished us in some way, but the next day we'd be back. He was a little more forgiving with me since my father was doctor to the lung patients (in other words, nearly all the guests) at the Sierras, so I enjoyed a bit more indulgence. Nevertheless, if I behaved badly, he would throw me out as well.

During the summer season, life began in the morning at the hotel pool. It was a fantastic 25-meter Olympic pool with lanes and a 2-meter diving board, used by Ernesto from a very young age, partly because he liked it, but also to show—something he did at every opportunity—that he wasn't afraid of anything, as well as to impress the girls. We'd dare each other and act like bigshots to see who could swim underwater longest, sometimes swimming nearly two lengths—that's 50 meters! One time, Roberto, who was younger, decided to copy us, but at about half-way he ended up floating; Ernesto's father raced into the pool to rescue him. I remember the scolding we got later that day when Roberto was already at home recovering with an icepack on his head.

Ernesto went to the Sierras with both his parents, while I was always accompanied by just my mother since my father was attending his patients. There were swimming classes where we first learned and then perfected our strokes with Argentine sports stand-outs the likes of the Espejo Pérez brothers and El Gringo Giordano. Ernesto and I were good swimmers, both winners in butterfly and breaststroke. When we were teenagers, his father trained us for an important swim meet with his eyes on beating the Argentine record for the under-15 age-group in the 100-meter breaststroke. We spent the entire summer training—Mr. Guevara taught us how to take the laps without losing valuable seconds. Ernesto was actually a more likely candidate to win than I was based on how he was looking in training. Finally the day of the meet arrived, we took our marks and were off, but at about 50 meters, out of the corner of my eye I saw Ernesto stop; I didn't know what had happened, but they were all yelling at me to keep swimming. I finished the last lap and broke the record, but it was a bittersweet victory. Ernesto had had an asthma attack in the water and that was why he couldn't finish the race. Good sportsman and as proud as he was, he came to congratulate me.

At siesta time, we weren't allowed to go near the Sierras—Celentano wouldn't allow us in because he said we bothered the highbrow guests while they either slept or played cards, dice or chess in the different lounge areas in the hotel. Only when the sun began to go down were we allowed back in to listen to a small orchestra that played waltzes, boleros and fox-trots on the patio where there was also dancing. As children, we only spied and laughed at the older boys who were already courting girls. And we went to the game rooms. Ernesto was a great chess player and could beat all of us except Negro Figueroa, Carlitos' older brother—there were some memorable matches between the two!

It was another story altogether once we began to wear long pants—as long as you were in short pants, you didn't have much right to anything. So this was when we began to go to the dances, decking ourselves out as best we could; if you were lucky enough to have a white jacket, you were a hit. But Ernesto never cared a thing about clothes and we teased him for wearing whatever he could lay his hands on. In those days, it was common for most of our clothes to be handed down from one relative to another. Ernesto inherited clothes from an uncle of

Ernesto with his gang of "scruffy" friends. From the very start, he frequented all types of social settings. Just as he enjoyed friendships with high-class friends, he lived endless adventures with the children of poor families. In this photo, Ernesto (as always, in the wool vest and long sleeves) poses with the Martín brothers (Enrique and José), the Ávalos (Manolo and el Negro), Fernando Romero, Juan Míguez, Cacho, and his brother and sister, Roberto (to the right) and Ana María.

his that were always too big and that he never went to the trouble to have altered. He'd put something on and ask, "You like what uncle so-and-so sent me?"

"You look like crap," I'd say.

"Who cares—I'm wearing it anyway."

Despite this "who cares" look of his along with his lousy dance skills, Ernesto had a way with the girls even in early adolescence when our romances were more imaginary than real—it was all 'I think so-and-so likes you' or 'don't look now, she's looking at you.' We liked them all, we asked them all to dance, but that was it— just *festejos*, our word for flirting in those days. Ernesto was so sure of himself, he didn't need fancy clothes or skill on the dance floor—he had incredible self-confidence. We gave him a hard time about the dancing, because he just had no ear for music whatsoever, but he ended up using it to his advantage. The girls thought it was cute and they'd say, "Oh, Ernestito, you poor thing, you don't know how to dance. Why don't you come over to my house and I'll teach you how." So off he went for afternoon tea, having a great time, eating everything they put on the table and, of course, never learning a thing because he had ears full of cotton.

The afternoon teas, the *guitarreadas*[11], playing *truco*[12], ping-pong, the barbecues, hikes in the hills, swimming in the creeks, riding horses—these were our summertime days in Alta Gracia, both for the "permanent cast" and the summer visitors. Many of the get-togethers were held in the houses of the girls in our group, because it was a way for the mothers to feel they had more control. One thing that Ernesto and I hated were the sing-alongs, since we both had an awful ear for music; whoever knew how to play the guitar and sing was instantly popular with the girls.

"Look at how that guy has them all eating out of his hand just because he can play, and he's just a midget … ," we'd whisper to each other as we watched in envy how all the girls had their eyes glued on some little guy playing boleros.

We preferred horseback riding, because it allowed us to stand out compared to the porteños who didn't have the experience we did on horseback. For us, porteño was an insult synonymous with snob. Ernesto, Carlitos Figueroa and I could show off doing tricks like rearing the horse up on its hind legs, and out in the hills it was

---

11 Guitar sing-alongs.
12 Popular card game.

easier to find secluded places, away from the parents' watchful eyes, to steal a kiss from a girl you liked.

The adults also had their own "elegant" versions of fun, most of British influence like fox-runs, golf and tennis. But the frosting on our summers was the three famous carnival celebrations: one in Villa Allende, one in La Cumbre and the third in Alta Gracia. As teenagers, we went to all three and the festivities could end up in brawls, depending on how things went with the other groups of revelers. The parties were organized by the big hotels in each town and, in order to not spend much, we'd go early and hide our bottles of gin in the bushes. We'd take a drink when no one was looking, so nobody could figure out how we ended up so smashed without money for drinks! Many of us were thrown out feet first, but not Ernesto; he was always more tempered with his drinking, although he did like to drink.

With the summer's end, the vacationers took the Rayo de Sol back to Buenos Aires and Alta Gracia went back to its small-town pace, its empty houses and wide-open spaces. For weeks our summer adventures still echoed in the hills and those of us who stayed struggled with the feeling of having been left behind in a place that suddenly seemed too large, constantly retelling anecdotes, real or imaginary romances, pranks—everything that had happened that summer. In the fall, we returned to school. There were three primary schools in Alta Gracia, all of them public. Ernesto did not attend the first years of school due to his asthma; Celia took on the task of giving him the education he was not able to get by regularly attending classes like other kids. I suppose this must have been an important factor in his upbringing, allowing him more freedom with no set schedule, schoolmates, teachers, recesses or homework. He was only limited by the stubborn asthma that sometimes took days to subside. I often stopped by alone or with friends and Celia would nod in the direction of his room to let us know that he was having another bout. There he was, nearly always reading lying on his stomach, a position that helped him to breathe better; or playing chess with his father or one of his siblings. However, when he was well, his free daily routine allowed him to interact with other children in Alta Gracia who didn't attend school for different reasons. They were from the poor families that worked the land or were caddies or porters. They weren't permitted inside the Sierras Hotel nor were they invited to tea or any of the summertime celebrations, but Ernesto spent the rest of the year with them and considered them just as much his friends as the children from wealthier families. He also learned things from them, such as the value of work. Ernesto's family always got a laugh recalling the time he went with his friends to harvest wild grapes in the country—they were paid 40 cents for eight hours of work, the equivalent of a couple of sandwiches. But they worked because they had to; Ernesto worked for fun. The thing was, ever faithful to his habit of devouring any kind of food, he ate more grapes than he harvested and ended up with a colossal case of diarrhea!

Another of our friends, Zacarías, who was four or five years older, was quite a character in Alta Gracia. Since no one knew his last name, we had christened him Tajamar in name of the town's famous reservoir. Zacarías went around with a basket selling *alfajores*[13] made by the woman who had adopted him.

"Hey, Zacarías, give me an alfajor on my tab," Ernesto or I would always chide him.

"No way," he'd say, "you owe me such-and-such and you don't have a tab!"

---

13 Argentine cookies.

The grade sheet from our fifth-grade class in the Manuel Solares school, 1940. With an average of 5.15, Ernesto did not stand out as a good student; however, the laxness was general—I barely scraped by with a 5.84 and we all got bad marks in conduct. With the exception of two, everyone else got "Needs Work". Ernesto, whose name was misspelled as Guevara Linch, received his best grades in Reading, History and Geography, interests he would maintain throughout his life. His asthma is also clearly evident in the grade sheet with a total of 68 excused absences.

Then one of us would distract his attention and the other would come from behind and grab a cookie or two and we'd take off running, splitting our sides with laughter and eating our booty while Zacarías cursed us up and down. Then, when he showed up to complain to our parents of the crime, our parents would wearily pay what was owed. We gave him a hard time, but he was still our friend. Whenever we organized an impromptu game, if he happened to pass by with this basket, we always called him to play and he'd drop what he was doing to join in. A few years later, he got a job grooming the tennis courts at the Sierras and became so full of himself, "Watch out, yous," he would say, "now I'm the boss around here!"

When Ernesto finally began to attend school regularly, we were classmates in fifth grade in Manuel Solares, a public school for boys. Ernesto was in the spotlight from the start. He arrived in the "the clunker" —the name we had given the Guevaras' old convertible Dodge—which always had clusters of children hanging like grapes from the bumpers. Celia, so easygoing, gave a ride to all the kids who wanted one. Another notable difference about the Guevara children was that they were exempt from the religion class. In those times, religion was still taught as an elective in public schools, but the truth is everyone attended with the exception of the occasional Jew. But the Guevaras had their own ideas. Ernesto's father was strictly atheist, having been raised that way, while Celia had attended an exclusive Catholic school and had her religious side. Every so often, she would experience a moment of religious fervor and her husband would give her a hard time. But the truth is she had a really awful relationship with the church priests. The Alta Gracia sacristan once brought to her attention the fact that she had come to church wearing a skirt without stockings, a sacrilege in those days. The sacristan, fat as a neutered cat, reprimanded her in front of everyone; Celia, as proud and arrogant as she was, reached under her skirt and stretched her transparent nylons with a triumphant smile. She swore she'd never go back.

Their children lived and breathed all that anti-clericalism, interpreting it in their own way. When they were older, they organized football matches between atheists and Catholics—quite a feat in a province as Catholic as Córdoba! Nevertheless, I believe the Guevara household was defined by clearly Christian principles. The children were always taught respect and solidarity with the needy, highlighting the terrible poverty in Alta Gracia at that time. Those lessons forged a sensitivity to suffering in Ernesto.

Ernesto's asthma kept him out of school often—his fifth grade attendance shows 68 excused absences. He was not a particularly good student and got even worse marks in conduct for all his showing off and antics aimed at making us laugh, like drinking ink or eating chalk. To be sure, he was just one more in a school full of boys who all wanted to stand out for being the naughtiest and most brazen. It's funny to look at the grade sheet—only two students received a "Good" in conduct, all the rest got "Needs Work". We were terrible, but it was all just childish pranks and boasting to make us feel more important than we were and to pass the time in a town where there was not much to do. Don Pancho Gutiérrez, who had a horse and mule cart he used for carrying small loads, had a much repeated saying. Whenever he would see a gang of us approaching to ask if we could borrow a horse or try one of his stews (that were fantastic), he would say, "One little boy, good little boy / two little boys, that's okay / three little boys, oh no,

I don't think so / three little boys, get the hell away!"
Because he knew that when we were in a pack, you
could be sure we were always up to no good—we even
made bets on who could pull off the biggest hoax. It was
a way to show bravery and Ernesto couldn't be beaten in
this; he was more than brave—he was fearless. He was
famous for his dives from "the wall". The wall was part
of an old well that the Jesuits had expanded and used as
a cistern. It was about three meters deep and was surrounded by rocks and trees. There were always idiots
jumping from the tree branches into the well.

Onc day as we were walking by it, Ernesto
announced, "I'm diving in."

"Don't be a jackass—you'll kill yourself," I told him.

"If so-and-so can do it, why not me?"

So the lunatic went and climbed to the highest
branch of a tree and stood on the end of it. The branch
swayed while we all waited to see what would happen.
It was dangerous—he was up really high, the well wasn't
large and it was full of rocks. I worried that if anything
happened to him, Ernesto's father would kill us. But he
jumped and came up breathing, so after that, he took
every opportunity to show off by diving in. Then
Zacarías Tajamar decided that he could do it as well, but
the difference was he didn't know how to swim, so once
he hit the water, we had to go in after him to save him
before he drowned.

Another way we passed the time was making fun of
the tourists—the snobby porteños, as we referred to anyone who wasn't Cordoban. For a laugh, we'd find out
whoever had rented horses and tell them, "Take the bit
out so the horse can spit." And when the poor bastards
removed it, the horses would take off for the stables, taking the corners at break speed with the tourists holding
on to the saddle for dear life!

46

A birthday party, possibly in the Guevara house. Here Ernesto and I appear again side by side. I, quite the little "man" already, am posing with my hand in my pocket. Ernesto continues to be the only one dressed in long sleeves. And debuting her shiny, new car (surely a birthday gift) is Ana María Guevara.

A page of doodles done by Ernesto that was given to me by the Office of Historical Matters during my last trip to Cuba. His typical irony was already apparent here; he writes: "Dear sirs: Having finally finished my studies this year, I plan to fully dedicate myself to drawing. Therefore, you may expect to receive samples of my work regularly from now on. Without further ado, Ernesto Guevara Serna." Below he adds: "Very highly esteemed student Serna."

This was life in Alta Gracia, the monotony of it broken only by international political events at the time. The Spanish Civil War affected us in significant ways, partly because of both our families' strident support of the Republic, but also due to the arrival in Alta Gracia of certain notable figures in exile from Spain. One of the most famous was the great composer Manuel de Falla, suffering from tuberculosis and under the care of my father, who quickly became part of the town's social life. He often repeated that he would not return to Spain as long as those who had killed his son-in-spirit, the poet Federico García Lorca, remained in power. Another family that quickly became friends of ours was that of Dr. Juan González Aguilar, a doctor who had had an important position in the Ministry of Health under the Republican government. His children, Carmen, Paco, Juan and Pepe, soon became part of our gang. Their house was a constant source of stories and facts related to the civil war that we soaked up like water. Both the González Alguilar and De Falla households often received visitors in exile, such as the poet Rafael Alberti.

Ernesto was only nine or ten at the time, but he was amazed by the stories of that war so far away yet seemingly so close. He had gotten his hands on a map of Spain and, through the news he got from the radio and from the Republicans in exile, he went about marking Republican advances on the map with little flags. Ernesto, even as a child, had a sort of passion for the military, not in the sense of order and obedience, but in terms of strategy and ability to command. He came up with the idea of a game that was to become one of our favorites; it consisted of making war trenches with dirt, rocks or whatever else we could find. We would form two teams and fire on each other with our "ammo" made of the fruit from a nearby tree—small, hard balls with a milky liquid inside. Then once, already a teenager, he showed his skill by a throwing a whizzing firecracker under the table at a Christmas dinner celebration in the house of a very important Alta Gracia family. There was a tremendous hullabaloo and Ernestito got a historic comeuppance. Who knows if he might not have recalled that episode after he became Che in the Sierra Maestra when he invented a homegrown system for setting off grenades with a fuse.

The Second World War also played a role in Alta Gracia and our lives. By then we were already teenagers and we lived this period in more awareness and participated more actively. Just like our parents, we were completely on the side of the Allies and any protest, appeal, petition or committee that was organized, we were right there in front. In contrast to the divisions that occurred during the Spanish Civil War in which there were supporters of Franco as well as Republicans, in WWII it was shameful to openly admit being a Nazi, so our position was right in line with most everyone's in Alta Gracia.

Toward the end of the war, a new movement was on the rise—this time in Argentina—that would shake the foundations of the country and divide it in two: Peronism. We, however, were already twenty-something by that time and had left the golden years in Alta Gracia far behind us. We now lived in Buenos Aires, 750 kilometers away from the town of our childhood.

That was when Ernesto dropped by my house one day nearly a year after that first unabashed proposal and, shaking his university grade report in my face, said, "Here it is, man. So I wasn't going to pass, was I? Start packing, Calica—we're going for real now."

CHAPTER 2

Departure

The name of the sidekick has changed from Alberto to Calica, but the trip is the same: two free-spirits spanning out over South America not knowing exactly what they're looking for or which way is north.

—ERNESTO GUEVARA

That departure so full of people, intermittent crying, the strange gaze of the people in second class staring at all the fine clothes, the leather jackets, etc., gathered to send off two odd-looking snobs loaded with luggage. The name of the sidekick has changed from Alberto [Granado] to Calica, but the trip is the same: two free-spirits spanning out over South America not knowing exactly what they're looking for or which way is north.[1]

The two snobs are us: Ernesto and I—two young, middle-class men with an uncertain destiny, high expectations and very little money. I'm the sidekick, Calica, 24 years old, no profession and only a high school diploma. Thus recalls Ernesto with typical irony in his trip log that cold afternoon of July 7, 1953 when we took the train from Retiro Station in Buenos Aires and headed into the unknown. He was 25 years old and just graduated from medical school.

His acid humor hides other things that went on that day: intense feelings barely shown, very much the Guevara style. That was the family way; they were very affectionate people who really loved each other, but were not demonstrative about it. There was little physical affection in their house and tears were frowned upon. But that day was special and there was an emo-

1 Ernesto Che Guevara, *Otra vez. El diario inédito del segundo viaje por América Latina (1953-1956)*, Buenos Aires, Sudamericana, 2000, p. 11.

tionally charged atmosphere laced with sadness among those that had come to see us off. Our departure was an important event and everyone was there: close and distant relatives, friends, old girlfriends and new "contenders". Since neither of us had an official girlfriend at the time, but there were several contenders in the running, there was some risk of a scene at the station, but we couldn't very well prevent them from coming to say good-bye. We were on our way and at that point nothing much else mattered. As Ernesto mentions, there were plenty of leather coats, good suits, custom-tailored clothes and high heels. The contrast was shocking compared to the rest of the setting, which consisted mainly of poor, indigenous people returning to their homeland after working in the city; they wore ponchos, carried their *guaguas*[2] on their backs and brought chickens, parakeets, their mate and kettle and their dogs and cats. In the 50's, clothing had still not become classless, so what people wore patently revealed social differences. There was no doubt that our farewell committee caused us to stand out in the second-class car with its wooden seats, but the ticket cost half as much as first-class and we had to stretch our meager savings as much as possible if we wanted to reach our final destination of Venezuela.

And our friends and relatives had not come empty-handed either; we boarded the train with an extra fifteen or so little packages and bundles of sweets, cookies, biscuits, drinks and other delicacies they had brought us for the journey. We did our best to stuff all this into the luggage rack where our two suitcases alone barely fit; Ernesto's, that weighed a ton due to all the books he had brought, and mine full of *pilchas*[3]. Just as Ernesto couldn't

----

2 Babies.
3 Clothes.

do without his books, ("I brought a few books I'm read-ing," he said when I commented that his suitcase was as heavy as lead), for me clothes were of absolute necessity when it came to getting a job, lodging, girls ... I wore my new tall boots from the López Taibo shop, a gift from my grandfather that were my pride and joy and accom-panied me throughout the journey. Ernesto, on the other hand, wore ankle boots and fatigues—he looked like a conscript. His brother Roberto, who was doing his *colim-ba*[4] at the time, had managed to get the fatigues "on loan" from the barracks and they were durable and warm—ideal for our trip.

Our mothers chatted slightly apart from the rest of the group, offering mutual consolation. Celia and Dolly had to say goodbye to us without knowing whether they'd ever see us again. I have no doubt they were worried, but they didn't cry. Celia came up to me and, looking me straight in the eye, said very seriously, "Take good care of Ernestito." When I saw the film *Motorcycle Diaries*, I was moved by the scene in which Mercedes Morán, who splendidly portrays Celia, asks Granado to take care of her son. It transported me back to that day in the station when she asked the same of me. I embraced her and promised her I would do just that. Meanwhile, my mother was saying to Ernesto, "You have more exper-ience traveling, so take care of Calica—he hasn't fully left the nest." And to me, she implored, "Please be care-ful, don't go around drinking—if you get drunk and end up in a fight, you could get yourself killed." At least they didn't seem to be too concerned about food, since they knew that Ernesto and I were capable of eating rocks or even grass. They had raised us that way: you couldn't be picky at the table, we ate what was served.

---

4 Military service.

Boarding time finally arrived and we took our seats after bidding everyone farewell. Ernesto's father recalls this moment in his book, when he uttered an enigmatic and providential sentence just before we got on the train: "Off goes a soldier of America!"[5] I don't remember it, but amid all the hugs, advice, kisses and crying, I could easily have missed it. Or perhaps I heard it and didn't give it much thought, took it as just another joke given his military attire. I joked about that, "Any minute, you're going to get thrown in jail and there'll be some officer saying, 'What's your name, soldier?' and ordering you to hit the dirt."

It was almost nightfall when the train finally pulled out. We leaned out the window to wave to all the dear faces we would not see again for so long. The train started out slowly as Celia walked along the platform with Carlos Figueroa. She picked up her pace along with the train as it gained speed and irreversibly headed into the distance. We saw her for the last time at the end of the platform. Much later I learned from Figueroa that at that moment she had burst into tears. She cried on the shoulder of her son's friend, then pulled herself together and rejoined the group that had already begun to disperse.

We settled into our seats, if one could use the word 'settle' to describe what you do in wooden seats as uncomfortable as those were. We were both reflective and sat in silence. The whole send-off, the day that so quickly turned to night, the suburbs of Buenos Aires that we watched transform into countryside—this all combined to create a certain nostalgia that neither of us would have acknowledged. Just to do something, I opened one of the packages full of cookies from the El

---

5 Ernesto Guevara Lynch, ...*Aquí va un soldado de América*, Buenos Aires, Sudamericana-Planeta, 1987, p. 7.

Ernesto, now a teenager, poses in front of the bus he rode from Alta Gracia to Córdoba every day to attend Deán Funes high school. The group is posing as the soccer team they would become when they challenged another group that made the same route by train. Among others in the photo are Beto Losada (the young man who tried to collect the rent from Ernesto's father), Chichín Carnelutti and the notary, Adolfo Barceló.

Molino café. They didn't make for much of a dinner, even less so the chocolates that Ernesto unwrapped from another package. We began to eye the casseroles, empanadas and other simple meals our train companions were taking out—much more satisfying foods at dinnertime than all our care-packages full of sweets. In fact, one of the advantages of traveling second class was that you were allowed to bring your own food to avoid the cost of the dining car. Finally the guy sitting next to us said, "Want some?", and offered us a chicken leg.

"Sííí!" we both said at the same time and in five minutes we had made friends with everyone in our car. We opened our fancy packages to share with everyone else. Some looked curiously at the pastries, since they had never tried them before. In exchange, they shared their food with us, showing us the warmth and solidarity of the people of the land that we would encounter so many times along the way.

With our bellies full and the sensation of having blended into the surroundings, our enthusiasm returned. We took out the map and went over our itinerary. The first stop would be La Quiaca where the General Belgrano line ended. From there, we would pass over into Bolivia, a country that neither of us had ever visited. It was Ernesto's idea to go to Bolivia.

"Instead of going via Chile, like I did with El Petiso [Granado], let's go through Bolivia, what do you say?" he had suggested when we first sat down with the map to plan the itinerary. Bolivia attracted us for two reasons, the first of which was basically tourist in nature: we dreamed of seeing Lake Titicaca because, in addition to being the highest lake in the world and a natural wonder, the Isla del Sol with its fantastic Incan ruins was located there. Ernesto had returned from his first journey through Latin America fascinated with the indigenous cultures that had reigned on the continent before the arrival of the Spaniards and had read a great deal on the subject. He always talked about the sense of futility and anguish he had experienced once he saw the contrast between the remnants of that glorious indigenous past, such as Machu Picchu, and the modern reality lived by the descendents of those people: poverty, discrimination and oppression.

The other reason was strictly socio-political. At that moment in time, Bolivia was the only white elephant in a Latin America infested with military dictatorships and authoritarian governments. There was Manuel Odría in Perú, Gustavo Rojas Pinilla in Colombia, Marcos Pérez Jiménez in Venezuela, Alfredo Stroessner in Paraguay, and pariahs the likes of Fulgencio Batista in Cuba, Anastasio Somoza in Nicaragua, Papa Doc in Haiti and Héctor Trujillo in the Dominican Republic—men who were practically overseers for the North American companies in those countries, the henchman of imperialism. And in Argentina, although we had a democratic government, it was a hard democracy if you weren't a Peronist. So we were thirsty for freedom, an asset for the conquering—it wasn't something that was served up on a silver platter. In Bolivia, however, the MNR (National Revolutionary Movement) had just triumphed over the dictatorship and there was a social revolution in the making. The first measures passed by the new government were encouraging: nationalization of the mines, the beginnings of agrarian reform and dissolution of the army which was inefficient and corrupt.

For two young socialist sympathizers like us, this was music to our ears. And apparently the feeling was mutual, because it was the only country for which we were able to easily obtain an entry visa. With only a bit more difficulty, we got one for Perú as well.

Getting the visa was the most complicated part of organizing the trip aside from financing it, which was another thorny matter. But in the worst case, we would have gone anyway without cash; however, there was no way to enter a country without a visa. Ernesto was an expert after his last trip, so he took care of the ordeal of obtaining the much sought-after permits in the consulates. We got the run-around at every turn; the dictatorships did not look kindly upon two penniless young men with plans to enter their countries without roundtrip tickets purchased in advance. We even had to get a health certificate issued by the Ministry of Health and another one of "good conduct" from the police.

The countries included on our itinerary were Bolivia,

Perú, Ecuador, Colombia and Venezuela. If getting a visa for the rest of them was a feat, the most difficult by far was Venezuela and that was the most important—we had to get in—because it was the whole purpose of the trip. Venezuela, however, was the main event of late for people from all over the Americas and Europe who wanted to work in that country where petroleum generated so much wealth. Luckily, we both had friends and family eager to help who provided us with connections in the different consulates. One relative gave us a contact in the Venezuelan consulate, thanks to which we were granted a personal interview. So there we went with our best "tuxes"—in other words, the best hand-me-down suit we could find. ("I'm wearing the 'Jorge'", Ernesto joked in reference to the uncle who had passed the suit on to him, and that was obviously not his size.) The consul received us, a big mulatto guy with a belly that was most likely the product of lots of liquor and good living.

"Well, gentlemen, what can I do for you?" he said after the standard protocol salutations.

"We wanted to request a visa to enter Venezuela. My friend here, who is a doctor, and I, nearly finished with medical school," I lied, "are about to set out on a journey through Latin America to study the fight against leprosy." This I recited nearly verbatim from the speech we had prepared in the Guevara's kitchen the day before.

"And the final destination of our trip is Venezuela, where I have a job practically guaranteed as a doctor in the La Guaira leper colony," added Ernesto with confidence.

"Do you have roundtrip tickets to Venezuela?" he asked.

"No, we don't have return tickets because we don't intend to return—we're going to stay in Venezuela to work," answered Ernesto while I thought, Or tickets to get there either, for that matter.

"Well, you know that in order to enter Venezuela, you must have return tickets. You have to guarantee that you will leave the country to obtain the tourist visa," insisted the consul as if he hadn't heard what we said.

"But I don't plan to leave—I'm going to stay and work in Venezuela!" exclaimed Ernesto, while I sunk into my chair and understood why his rugby teammates had given him the nickname Fuse, short for "Furious de la Serna".

"You, sir, cannot do that; you *must* return to Argentina because to practice medicine in Venezuela, you have to revalidate your degree," asserted the consul, raising his voice at least two notches.

"But listen, we're going to contribute to science in Venezuela ..."

"You will not enter Venezuela and our conversation is over," the consul cut him off.

"I am going to Venezuela and I'm going to stay...!"

"...Over my dead body you are!" yelled the consul, who by then had turned completely red, or at least as red as a mulatto can get.

"No, not over your dead body," replied Ernesto, recovering his composure, "I'm going to enter the country by stepping on your fat belly!" Predictably, he threw us out at that point and, of course, we could forget about the visa. I couldn't believe what I had just witnessed and mentally, I bid farewell to my dreams of the good life in the Venezuelan Caribbean.

"Are you out of your mind?! How could you talk that way to the guy who was supposed to grant us the visa!" I reproached Ernesto.

"He wasn't going to give it to us anyway. Relax, Calica, we'll figure out a way eventually. Once we're there, we'll get across the border one way or another."

And that was how it went: one way or another, we somehow managed to get what we wanted.

So there we were, in our second-class seats with the idea of crossing five countries to get to the opposite end of South America, our only assets being an entry visa for Bolivia, another for Perú and a very modest allowance that I held under my waistband. My mother, who was a horrible cook but a fantastic seamstress, had made me a sort of cloth belt with a pocket for keeping our cash that I wore underneath my pants, much like those that are sold today for travelers. Ernesto had dubbed it the "chastity belt". There I held all the money that we had been able to scrounge from our relatives. "Consider it a loan," more than one had joked, "when you come back rich and famous, you can pay me back with interest." I had collected 7,100 pesos and Ernesto 6,900 which together didn't even amount to enough to buy a plane ticket to Venezuela. It was a meager sum, but we had sworn not to ask for more from our families no matter what happened. We would have to stretch those few pesos to last the entire trip. I had asked my mother for a very small sum that she most likely took great pains to eke out of what little we had been left after my father's death.

Ernesto had decided that I should be the one to carry the money in the chastity belt, because, according to him, I was much more organized about clothes. However, we were constantly arguing about it, because he was always asking me for *guita*[6] and it was a nuisance for me to have to find a bathroom so no one would see me every time I had to take money out. So I threatened him with resigning my job as team "banker" and giving him all the money. "No, no, it's alright, you keep carrying it," he said; despite all his experience traveling, he wasn't very skillful in the financial management department. On the trip with Granado, they had ended up

_____

6 Money.

Here we are, all grown up at 15, Ernesto and I with our arms around each other's shoulders posing at the Hotel Sierras pool. Our summertime gang is with us, from left to right: Oscar Salduna, Rafael Cazenave, Lino Palacios (son of the notable illustrator who summered in Alta Gracia), Tito Pérez (standing), Chichita Raedemaker, Ginger Griffiths, Carlitos Figueroa and Freddy Lahitte.

broke very early on, so there was nothing to manage, no funds to hide. That is, except for the famous 15 dollars that his girlfriend Chichina had given him to buy her a bathing suit in the United States and who knows where he kept them hidden, but that he managed to conserve until the end.

For lack of monetary resources, we carried a different kind of capital in our suitcases: the letters of recommendation that we had been given by friends and relatives to people who could be of help to us in the different countries along the way. We had dozens of them; everyone supported our idea to travel, immediately remembering acquaintances that wouldn't mind helping us if we needed it. Ernesto, who had more experience with this type of thing, explained to me that it was good to have someone to turn to if you were dying of hunger, needed a good bath or a contact to help with red tape. Our families also helped with donations of clothing, so nearly all we took were on loan or hand-me-downs; in this sense, we were well-provisioned.

As the night drew on, the crying of babies began to subside and the laughter to die down. Even the parakeets were silenced. So, as uncomfortable as we were leaning against each other, we began to nod off. Fortunately, being so young meant that sleep always had the upper hand over discomfort. And we were exhausted, not only from the emotional farewell and last-minute preparations, but from the string of farewell parties our friends had organized that all went on until the wee hours and had left our livers in a deplorable state. The night before our departure, the two of us went with Carlos Figueroa to have dinner at a club on Santa Fe Avenue. I wore my best suit—a stripped, double-breasted jewel—the only one that wasn't second-hand, custom-tailored for me in the glory days when my father was still alive. And of course we drank a lot, mainly Carlos and I, since Ernesto was more moderate when it came to alcohol. We started in with the same old number as always whenever we had one drink too many, in raised voices, "To hell with Perón!" Someone always took offence, grabbed their gloves and came over to confront us and it always came to blows, which I must admit, I relished. I've spent many a night at the police station for this type of thing. That night, the minute I started with the Perón insults, a guy from Tucumán came around looking for a fight and I told the others, completely self-confident, not to get involved, that I'd take care of him.

So out we went. I remember that they were taking up the streetcar tracks at the time and the minute we started fighting, the other guy gave me a head-butt and laid me out in all my height right in the construction ditch. I was completely done for and my suit was in a miserable state. "So we shouldn't get involved, right?" joked Ernesto, as they helped me out between fits of laughter. My poor mother spent the rest of that night trying to clean the suit so I could take it with me the following day, since it was the best I had.

Juvenile bravado aside, anti-Peronism was a serious thing that we inherited from our families and that divided all of Argentina in the 1950's. Both the Guevara family and mine saw Perón as the incarnation of fascism in Argentina and felt their opposition to Peronism to be a logical extension of their support for the Spanish Republican government, the Allies in the Second World War and for socialism. Our parents collaborated the minute any committee was organized against Perón. In the Guevara house, it was an everyday thing to hear Ernesto's father rant against Peronism and swear that armed clashes would break out any moment. There was no way to contradict him or to say anything in favor of Peronism—it was strictly forbidden. And the same thing went for my house. It was a very close-minded stance that was common at the time that you simply could not credit Peronism with anything positive, not even the undeniable social advances—this our families attributed to the socialists. They would say, "That was already invented by the socialists—Palacios presented the proposal for such-and-such law." Although true, it was no less true that the Peronists were the first to actually put said social principles into practice. Ernesto and I, just like nearly all our friends, took our parents' view; we felt we had no freedom. We were even told not to criticize the government in front of the maid for fear that she might report us. Despite whatever social progress may have been achieved, the lack of political and civil liberties held more weight with us.

Ernesto and I used to go out just before elections to put up anti-Perón posters. Once we began university, the anti-Peronist sentiment was reinforced because all the university associations in Córdoba were in opposition as well. So when we set out on our trip, Ernesto and I were both self-declared anti-Peronists. And although Ernesto had not yet become a Marxist, he did have socialist ideas. He was not indifferent to poverty or to the social drama going on in the country at that time: the hunger, unemployment and injustices generated by social distinctions. The awkwardness he had to live through every summer when his best friends were not allowed to step foot in the Hotel Sierras, the profound social crisis he discovered along his travels on motorbike through the provinces of Argentina, his many readings and the tour around the rest of Latin America with Granado all influenced his ideas. When he returned from that trip, he even began to acknowledge some good things about the Peronist government, saying that, after having seen poverty up close, it was easier to understand the Peronist voters. This demonstrates Ernesto's sensitivity and capacity for reflection, because at that time all our families and friends were unequivocally, blindly opposed to Peronism. He, however, was always developing his own very unique critical thinking. During our university years, many other friends and I were militantly active in various student political parties and leftist groups. I tried to encourage Ernesto to participate, but he preferred not to take sides then; he did, however, have political and particularly ethical opinions about the world from a more existentialist

Ernesto's visa entry for Venezuela during his first trip through Latin America with Alberto Granado in 1952. This copy was given to me as a gift in Cuba. The original is conserved in the Office of Historical Affairs there.

point of view, more derived from direct experience with social realities. This is why his trips were such defining moments in his ideological development. They weren't about tourism or adventure—they were the fire that forged a revolutionary mind that would later change the world. At the end of his travel journal from the first trip, Ernesto makes an annotation in the margin referring to a "revelation" that came to him in a conversation in a mountain village with a man "whose only visible teeth were the four incisors." It is startling to read, in light of what would later occur, what my young friend could already make out of his future:

Now I knew… I knew that, the moment the great

governing spirit strikes the blow to divide all humanity into just two opposing factions, I would be on the
side of the *pueblo*[7], and I know this because I saw it
written in the stars that I, the eclectic dissector of
doctrines, psychoanalyst of dogmas, howling like a
madman, will jump barricades or trenches, stain my
weapon in blood and, in my rage, slash as many
enemy throats as I can get my hands on. And I can see,
as if a deep fatigue had overcome my recent exal-
tation, how I sacrifice myself to the authentic leveling
revolution, declaring *mea culpa* in my martyrdom.

I can already feel my nostrils open and smell the
acrid scent of gunpowder and blood, of enemy death;
my body at attention, ready to fight, I prepare myself
like some sacred place for the resounding echo of the
new vibrations and hopes of the triumphant proletariat's bestial howling.[8]

The train whistle woke us the following morning,
along with the parakeets that began to scream once again.
We had arrived in the city of Córdoba. The ground was
white with the heavy frost that had fallen over night. Our
dear friends Mario Salduna and Raúl Tisera were waiting
for us on the platform, trembling with cold. In their desire
to take part in our trip in some way, they had brought us
a baked chicken and two liters of cheap wine—at seven in
the morning! Both were old friends from Alta Gracia, so
saying goodbye to them was a bit like bidding farewell to
the town of our childhood and adolescence. We were
only 36 kilometers away and I was sorry we couldn't go
for a visit. When we were planning the trip, I had suggested to Ernesto, "What if we stop for a couple of days in

---

7 Common people.
8 E. Guevara, *Diarios de motocicleta*, p. 208.

Alta Gracia? It's along the route to La Quiaca ..."

"No, you're crazy; if we go to Alta Gracia, we'll never leave, we'll end up spending a month eating and drinking, going from one dinner invitation to the next and adios trip," Ernesto responded.

And he really was right—Alta Gracia was like a magnet for us. We hadn't lived there for many years, but it continued be our "place in the world" and whenever we could, we'd go for a visit. The summer before our trip, while Ernesto crammed for exams, I went with Carlitos Figueroa to stay for four months in his family's empty house there. We had earned a bit of money together from the sale's commission on a piece of property and decided to go spend it in Alta Gracia. Of course, the money didn't last very long so we shared our hunger instead. We renamed the house *Los Galgos*, the greyhounds, in honor of how thin we were. But they were fantastic months, full of parties every day and night. We got ourselves invited to lunch or tea in girls' houses and managed to keep going that way. We had only one white dinner jacket to wear out at night, so we took turns with it. We also put up any friends who came to spend a weekend or night. Ernesto escaped whenever he could from Buenos Aires and would come for a couple of days. There wasn't as much as a crust of bread in the house and our hunger was most acute when we came home from the nights of partying on an empty stomach. But there was always wine and gin. Whenever someone came to visit, they always brought a bottle that we rapidly dispatched. And there were the girls, of course—a constant parade of gorgeous creatures.

At that time, both Ernesto and I lived in Buenos Aires and, despite the variety of distractions and social activities offered by a big city, we continued to prefer the charm of Alta Gracia that symbolized our carefree childhood years. Once we were teenagers, things began to change and we slowly grew away from that small mountain paradise. Alta Gracia had no secondary school, so I was sent to board at the Colegio Lasalle in Argüello, Córdoba, where I suffered at the hands of the priests. On top of that my parents had separated, a shameful thing in those days, so I began a difficult phase of my life. Ernesto went to the Colegio Deán Funes in Córdoba, traveling to and from Alta Gracia daily at first; then the family moved to the city and left Alta Gracia. We both made new friends and lived out new experiences, but still saw each other on weekends, over winter vacation and, of course, all summer long in Alta Gracia. And many significant things continued happened to us in that cherished place of our upbringing.

Such as the summer I returned from school to happily find that we had taken on a young housemaid who was very pretty, about seventeen or eighteen, just slightly older than me. It was my opportunity for the long-awaited sexual debut. Things were that way then; we had been taught that "good" girls—daughters of our parents' friends—might allow an occasional stolen kiss, but no further! So sexual initiation had to occur either with "professionals", meaning you had to have money, or with a willing housemaid. And as luck would have it, the girl mamá had taken on, la Negra Rodríguez[9], was willing, so I thus had my first experiences with her. She was the daughter of the blacksmith who took care of our horses and I remember that every time I saw him working with his hammer, I thought, "He's going to take that hammer to my head". I felt that I had done something bad and went to church to confess my sins.

---

9 The surname is fictitious; although it has appeared in other biographies, out of courtesy to la Negra, I prefer to preserve her anonymity.

Partido Reformista

AFILIADO AL P. R. DE CÓRDOBA

VOTO PARA:

Presidente: Ricardo Wehbe
Secretarios: Eduardo Patrizi
             Emilio Gutierrez
             Néstor Massaro
             Carlos Ferrer
             Marcelo Getar
             Raúl Nieto

DELEGADOS DE CURSO

7°· Año Pedro Bonadero, Ermes Marcili
6°, ,,   Pedro Toselo, Oscar Asis
5°. ,,   Simón Pérez, Oscar Niño
4o. ,,   Carlos Ceballos, Carlos Serra
3°. ,,   Víctor Yunes, Juan Carlos Paoloni
2o. ,,   Carlos Silva, Raúl Mangia
1°. ,,   Hugo Olmos, Alejandro Centeno

DELEGADOS A F. U. C.

         Raúl G. Audenino, Oscar Niño
Suplentes: Emilio Gutiérrez
           Carlos Ferrer
           Luis Lencina

The voting ballot from the university elections that I have kept as a cherished souvenir from my days in the University of Córdoba Student Federation. Also on the ballot are my good friends from that time, whom I never saw again.

71

The priest scolded me, "What have you done, you irresponsible boy!"

Of course I fell into sin again every chance I could get and I constantly bragged about it to Ernesto and all my other envious friends. But then I went back to school and when I came home again, I discovered that my mother, who surely must have suspected something, had dismissed her. But to my surprise, Negra had found employment in none other than the Guevara house! The minute I saw Ernesto, his winning smile gave away everything—he had also debuted with Negra. During that vacation, I had to settle for my friend's stories, which were surely a little exaggerated. At that age, the most important thing—more than the actual sex—was to be able to tell your friends about it and prove that you were an expert. Ernesto made us laugh when he described how Negra, in the heat of the moment, would give him a drag on his inhaler so he could keep going despite the fits of asthma he had throughout. Over the years, we always fondly remembered Negra, who had so ably initiated us into an art that we later spent years perfecting. A long while after that when he was living in Buenos Aires, Ernesto took up with another household maid, Sabina. Although unattractive and older than Ernesto, she was nevertheless willing to satisfy the instincts of her employer's son. Ernesto was more practical than demanding in this sense and made the most of the occasion with whomever and whenever the opportunity presented itself.

But back then, sex was sex and courting was something else. The latter was reserved for the girls we dated, the ones with whom you couldn't even dream of going any further. The distinction between the two was categorical: they were the daughters of the well-known families of Alta Gracia, the friends of friends. Nothing ever went beyond courting and there was always a chaperone present—there was no question of being left alone. We liked them all, but there were a few special girls. As a young teenager, Ernesto and his cousin Negrita Córdova Iturburu had a crush on one another. And then there was the famous Chichina, whom he met through my brother Jorge who had taken him to her house in Villa Allende one day. Her family was very well-off.

The stories about Ernesto's visits to Chichina's house were always good for a laugh. He would finish a tennis match and, all sweaty with his hair in his face, sit right down at the fancy dining room table where good manners were the rule and guests were attended by waiters and a butler. Everyone would look horrified, probably thinking, Where in the world did he come from? That is, until someone asked him a question and he opened his mouth; he would amaze them all with his intelligence, his composure, how much he knew from having read so much and his articulate way with words. Then they would say, "What a clever boy," and forget all about the way he looked.

That relationship was cut short when he set out on the trip with Granado. It was good while it lasted, however I don't think Ernesto was nearly as smitten as many people said. In fact, our trip together began one year afterwards and he rarely mentioned her in all the months of days and nights we spent sharing stories, telling each other everything. "Remember so-and-so?" he'd say, "Well, blah, blah, blah happened with her." Half the time I had to cut him off and say, "Wait a minute—you already told me that one," and vice versa. So he had many opportunities to talk about her, but never did. I suppose either he had forgotten her already or he was bitter and didn't want to talk about her. Women he never lacked—he had a way with them. Even though he wasn't tall, he was attractive and had a handsome face; he was good at soccer, swimming and excellent on horseback; he was very well-read and had memorized a few verses to sweeten up the girls; and he was a Guevara de la Serna, which didn't hurt in the circles in which we moved. In other words, he was a first-division outstanding player.

The monotony of the journey across the country from south to north was lightened up thanks to our fellow travelers, friendly people with whom we shared lively conversations. The preferred topics were soccer and boxing. It was the golden era of boxing in Argentina and Ernesto was passionate about the sport, something he had inherited from his father who had taught him all the basic moves from an early age. I remember the afternoons spent in their yard with Mr. Guevara giving lessons to his boys and their friends. Since they only had one pair of gloves, he put us in pairs and gave the biggest boy the left glove (unless he was a lefty) and the right one to the smaller. He wrapped our free hands in rags and that was how we fought. When we were older and living in Buenos Aires, we spent a lot of time at Luna Park. At that time, there were two groups: those who were fans of "El Mono" Gatica and the others for Alfredo Prada. Ernesto and I would argue because he liked Prada, who had been asthmatic and lived in Alta Gracia. He also liked Oscar Pita because he was from Rosario. Even though Ernesto had barely lived there, since he was born in Rosario, he considered himself a native son of that city and saw everyone from there as special. Of course, he was also faithful in soccer—he was a devoted fan of the Rosario Central team. We often went to watch Torito Aguirre, a Rosario player that he really admired, who had a very complicated life but was

MINISTERIO DE EDUCACION
UNIVERSIDAD DE BUENOS AIRES
FACULTAD DE CIENCIAS MEDICAS

DECANATO

B.M.

Al señor Rector de la Universidad de Buenos Aires

Doctor Carlos A. Bancalari

Cúmpleme comunicar al señor Rector que el exalumno de **MEDICINA**

Don Ernesto Guevara .... ha sido aprobado en todos los exámenes requeridos para optar al diploma de **MEDIC O** el que corresponde le sea expedido.

Transcribo a continuación la planilla con los datos de identidad y clasificaciones obtenidas:

Nacido en Provincia de Santa Fé el 14 de Junio de 1928

Libreta de enrolamiento: Matrícula n° 6.460.503 Dist. Mil. 43 Reg. 41

Cédula de identidad n° – – – – – – – – Policía de la Capital. Of. Enrol. Córdoba

Libreta Cívica n° – – – – – – – – Ofic. – – – – – – Secc. – – – – – – – –

	ASIGNATURAS	CALIFICACIÓN	OFICIAL O LIBRE	FECHA	
1° CICLO	1° Anatomía Descriptiva	Bueno (1)	LIBRE	Abril	1948
	Anatomía Topográfica				
	2° Embriología e Histología	Aprobado		Agosto	1948
	Fisiología Fís. y Quím. Biológica	Aprobado	OFICIAL	Marzo	1949
	3° Parasitología	Bueno	"	Noviembre	1948
	Semiología y Clínica Propedéutica	Bueno	"	Abril	1950
2° CICLO	1° Anatomía y Fisiología Patológicas	Aprobado	LIBRE	Noviembre	1949
	Microbiología	Aprobado	LIBRE	Julio	1949
	Patología General y Médica	Aprobado	OFICIAL	Diciembre	1952
	Patología Quirúrgica	Aprobado	"	Setiembre	1951
	2° Técnica Quirúrgica	Aprobado	"	Noviembre	1951
	Toxicología	Bueno	"	Diciembre	1950
	Terapéutica y Farmacología	Aprobado	"	Diciembre	1950
3° CICLO	Clínica Otorrinolaringológica	Bueno	PROMOCION	Noviembre	1951
	Clínica Oftalmológica	Aprobado	"	Noviembre	1952
	Clínica Urológica	Prom.Aprobado	"	Noviembre	1952
	Clínica Ginecológica	Aprobado	"	Setiembre	1951
	1° Radiología y Fisioterapia	Distinguido	"	Setiembre	1951
	Clínica Psiquiátrica	Bueno	"	Octubre	1951
	Clínica Neurológica	Aprobado	"	Abril	1953
	Clínica Pediátrica y Puericultura	Bueno	OFICIAL	Octubre	1952
	Clínica Obstétrica (Fisiología)	Distinguido	"	Diciembre	1952
	Patología y Clínica de la Tuberculosis	Prom.Aprobado	PROMOCION	Diciembre	1952
	Clínica Dermatosifilográfica	Prom.Aprobado	"	Noviembre	1952
	Medicina Legal	Aprobado	OFICIAL	Diciembre	1952
	Higiene y Medicina Social	Bueno	"	Diciembre	1952
	2° Ortopedia	Aprobado	PROMOCION	Diciembre	1952
	Clínica Obstétrica (Patología)	Aprobado	OFICIAL	Diciembre	1952
	Clínica Médica	Distinguido	"	Abril	1953
	Clínica Quirúrgica	Aprobado	"	Diciembre	1952
	Patología y Clín. de las Enfer. Infec.	Distinguido		Diciembre	1952

Rindió su última asignatura el día 11 de Abril de 1953.–

Saludo al señor Rector muy atentamente.

Por ....

Dr. FEDERICO O. PINTARELLI
SECRETARIO

DR. JORGE A. TAIANA
DECANO

Ernesto's medical diploma, proof of the feat of having passed the 12 exams he had to take between Oct.1952, when he came back from the trip with Granado, and April 1953. This is the paper he shook in my face when he triumphantly announced that we could set out on our journey with the following words: "Here it is, man. So I wasn't going to pass, was I? Start packing, Calica—we're going for real now."

a great player. And even though he wasn't into horses as much as we Ferrer boys were, Ernesto did come to the races with us a few times, more for fun than anything else, since we were always counting pennies and could hardly make a bet. Of course, we watched all sporting events from the cheapest seats, which was all we could afford.

The Guevaras had moved to Buenos Aires just before Ernesto began medical school, after having lived for four or five years in the city of Córdoba. That was where he met Alberto Granado, the older brother of one his classmates, Tomás Granado. In Buenos Aires, they lived in a big—albeit somewhat run-down—house on Aráoz Street in the Palermo neighborhood. The house was a noisy parade of friends and family just like their houses in Alta Gracia and Córdoba had been, just not as happy. Some things were different. Ernesto's parents were separated in fact, although they continued to live in the same house; Celia suffered health problems, which I would later discover had been breast cancer, since illnesses were not discussed openly then and much less those of a female nature; and their financial woes also continued to accumulate.

Ernesto nearly always had some sort of job, even if was just part-time, to cover his expenses and help out at home. One of his schemes was bottling DDT with Carlos Figueroa in the Guevaras' garage and selling it to different building supervisors to kill cockroaches; they called it *Vendaval*[10]. They managed to save a few pesos from that venture, despite all the family's complaints about the unbearable smell. In the end, they had to shut down the business when they nearly became ill from breathing the fumes of that powerful insecticide. Ernesto also

---

10 Gale.

worked as an assistant to Dr. Salvador Pisani, the director of the Pisani Clinic where they did research into new therapies for treating allergies and asthma.

When we decided to make the trip, one of the objections of Ernesto's parents was that, if he stayed, the recommendation of Dr. Pisani—an eminent figure in the field—assured Ernesto a job as a doctor either in his clinic or some other. But then we all know what Ernesto thought about the security that most of us seek in life. His father sums up his sentiments regarding our decision to travel, which we interpreted then as just mumbled griping:

> Our illusions crumbled like a house of cards; we knew what awaited him and we knew it well. He would walk miles and miles, hop into any old truckbed, sleep wherever and eat whatever he could find. He wasn't remotely concerned about his asthma or his health in general and he'd go off wandering the world without a moment's thought for the dangers. As for us, his parents and siblings—there was nothing we could do, no way to intervene. He was no longer a child, he was now Dr. Ernesto Guevara de la Serna and he did what he wanted.[11]

The arrival of my family in Buenos Aires was no triumph either. My parents had separated while I spent my adolescence in boarding school. At nineteen, when I was already in medical school in Córdoba, my father died of a heart attack at age 47. My father, like the Guevaras, belonged to a social circle that believed that business was not suitable for our likes—the only appropriate jobs were professions (like law or medicine). So he had lived

---

11 Ernesto Guevara Lynch, *Mi hijo el Che*, La Habana, Editorial Arte, 1988.

very well thanks to his medical practice, but he had lived from one day to the next without ever thinking to invest the money. For example, he had only partially paid for a small farm close to Alta Gracia that we were forced to return to the owner after his death. So my mother and brothers had to move to a rented two-bedroom apartment on Salguero Street, just two blocks away from Guevaras' house on Aráoz. Not long after that, my quitting medical school led me to move into that small space as well. The proximity brought back the everyday nature of the old days to my friendship with Ernesto. On his way back from classes, he'd get off the bus on Sante Fé Street and stop by to ask my mother, "Dolly, what's for lunch?" If he liked what she was cooking, he'd stay; if not, he'd go on home. Those were hard times after having lived like kings in Alta Gracia in a classy house right on the Tajamar lake with two servants, a chauffer and a cook to end up in a small apartment we could barely keep up. My two brothers were studying and one of them, Chacho, also worked as a clerk in the Courts; as I mentioned before, I didn't have a job or studies and barely managed to do whatever occasional part-time work came my way. The tables were now turned and Ernesto's snobby friend was even more penniless than he was. But our group of Alta Gracia friends that now lived in Buenos Aires was always ready to help each other out, so whenever any of us had money in our pockets, we'd treat the rest to a night of dancing in the clubs or a drink. Or we'd lend each other a hand to go on a date with some "contender" or other and her friends. And if we didn't have a dime, there was always the Guevaras' kitchen table and their legendary after-dinner talks for entertainment; now that the children were grown, they were much more politicized and interesting. Celia kept up her habit of stretching

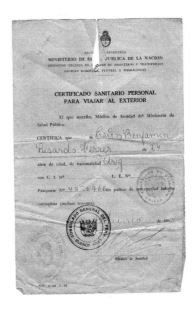

Traveling in 1953 in a Latin America plagued with dictatorships entailed arduous work before setting out: visas, certificates of health and good conduct and an up-to-date passport. Ernesto, more experienced in all this, organized our visits to all the government offices to get the paperwork done. Here is my first passport—it was the first time I had ever been out of the country.

the food to accommodate any number of diners. And Patatín, who was in charge of the cooking then, continued perfecting his one and only recipe: roast beef and potatoes!

Once on board the General Belgrano, that whole life in Buenos Aires seemed so far away now as I felt the train advance in a straight line toward a luminous future. Argentina bid us goodbye with the majesty of the towering summits that we could see from the Huamahuaca Divide. The train finally approached the end of the line: La Quiaca, the last town in Argentine territory.

"Surrounding the bald peaks, a grey mist adds tone and definition to the landscape. Laid out before us, a thin thread of water separates the territories of Bolivia and Argentina. On either end of a tiny railroad bridge, the two flags face each other."[12] This is the description Ernesto made in his journal that perfectly sums up the geography and atmosphere there. It was also the setting in which the worst thing that could have happened to Ernesto did: he had the most severe asthma attack I had ever seen.

I had witnessed lots of attacks before, but never like this. I thought he was going to die right then and there— I was desperate and didn't know what to do to help him. We hadn't even gotten off the train, I was paralyzed with fear, my friend was in agony, I had all the luggage to deal with and we had nowhere to go.

"Señor, can I carry those for you?" A bevy of little Indians appeared, all asking the same question, wanting to earn an easy tip in exchange for carrying our bags. I distributed the luggage and bundles left over without thinking whether I'd ever see them again amid the chaos of the station. I lifted Ernesto onto my shoulder and started asking desperately where to find the closest inn. I

---

12 E. Guevara, *Otra vez*, p. 11.

dragged him there, followed by the court of little guys who were carrying our luggage. Once in the inn, I stayed by his side while he continued gasping for air and watched how he agonized in that dive we had ended up in. A few hours went by and the attack finally began to subside. Once again, Ernesto had won out over his worst enemy. When it was all over, I scolded him just like a mother whose child has been in danger, relief mixed with anger.

"Are you crazy? How the hell is it that you didn't tell me what could happen and what to do in that situation?"

"You're right, Calica; next time you give me an adrenaline injection. But careful—in the muscle, not the vein; otherwise *me dejás seco*[13]. "

Nevertheless, we had to wait a whole day in that little town for Ernesto to completely recover. He spent that time drinking mate and eating rice, the only things he said his body could handle. He decided that excesses of food over the days prior to our departure—all the farewell parties combined with our victuals on the train—were the cause of the attack. The aridness of the landscape on top of the tedium of having nothing to do but wait made us a bit nostalgic—the notorious *morriña*[14] as my mother called it, a word that Ernesto loved; he used it citing her in one of his letters. The only thing that saved us was a chance encounter with an old friend from our Alta Gracia gang, Tiqui Vidoza, who was now a border patrol. The conversation and laughter brought back our enthusiasm and, partly as compensation for the bad time we'd had on the border and partly because of the good exchange rate we'd enjoy in Bolivia, I convinced Ernesto to get first-class tickets on the train to La Paz. He reluctantly agreed—we'd enter Bolivia in class.

---

13 You'll kill me.
14 Blues.

CHAPTER 3

Bolivia

I was born in Argentina, that's no secret. I'm a Cuban and an Argentine and, no offence to the illustrious sovereigns of Latin America, but I feel just as much a patriot of Latin America, of any Latin American country, and if necessary, I would be willing to give my life for the liberation of any of those countries without requests, demands or exploitation of anyone.

—Ernesto Guevara

In Villazón, the little Bolivian town where the train started out for La Paz, we bought our first-class tickets for even less than we had paid for the second-class seats we had on the trip to La Quiaca. We had crossed the border on July 10 with no complications other than the standard paperwork; our visas and passports were all in order. Ernesto was completely over the asthma and the altitude seemed to work wonders for him. During the train trip, he even abandoned his standard menu of rice and mate to enjoy meals in the dining wagon where the menu was so inexpensive for us. He also gave in to the temptation of the mysterious stews and exotic fruits brought in from the valleys and offered by the indigenous people at every station. Our first-class tickets put us in the tourist category, which meant we were deserving of all manner of attention from helpers anxious to receive a tip. When we first boarded the train, one of them—a really big guy—patronizingly took our bags. Ernesto stopped him short in that decisive way he had when he was angry. The colossus got the message that his "services" were not welcome and that he was not getting a tip out of us, so he finally let go of our bags.

Bolivia welcomed us with the same landscape we had already grown accustomed to in the final kilometers covered in Argentina—the omnipresent grey of the *altiplano* and the lack of vegetation. The only hint of color was the clothing worn by the Indians—their little hats, their ponchos and skirts—always in vivid colors. We were anxious to learn about the social changes afoot under the new revolutionary government. "Bolivia is a country that has set an important example for the rest of the Americas," Ernesto wrote enthusiastically in a letter describing our trip to Tita Infante, a friend from medical school. We imagined the masses of rebellious campesinos and miners. However, to our disappointment, the part of Bolivia we were crossing was barely populated. The few groups of people we encountered were nearly all indigenous, chubby, short and stocky all of them. It was strange to us that, despite the intense cold, their feet were bare except for the flip-flops they wore made of tire-rubber. We tried to talk to them at the station-stops, but they were clearly very reserved people that only spoke to answer direct questions, they seemed indifferent to everything and most didn't even speak Spanish—they spoke Quechua or Aimará. We would have to wait until we got to La Paz to find the real social upheaval we were looking for.

The atmosphere on the train was different. There were no indigenous people traveling in first class, only whites. Over dinner in the dining car, we made a contact that would prove truly useful during our stay in La Paz. We struck up a conversation with an Argentine who was about our age, José María Nougués, on his way to visit his father who was in exile in Bolivia. We immediately discovered that we had mutual friends in common—he knew some of Ernesto's rugby teammates and doctor friends of my father's. We spent the night in the first-class sleeper car, but even that couldn't protect us from the bitter cold. We awoke the next morning shivering— even the water in the toilets had frozen! The Indians remained unperturbed with their bare feet, their cheeks bulging with the wad of coca leaves they constantly chewed. Coca has an anesthetic effect—it dulls hunger,

The entry visa we were given by the Bolivian consulate in Buenos Aires. Our movements are recorded there: we arrived at the border town of Villazón on July 10 and were in La Paz by the 14th. Our departure from the country was stamped August 17 when we headed to Perú.

thirst, fatigue and sorrow. It was the natural antidote to counter the sad landscape we were crossing, melancholic as the tinkle of a distant pan flute.

It was still daytime, around four in the afternoon, when we saw the city of La Paz in the distance. It stretched out in the bottom of a gorge at the foot of the impressive Illimani peak, a white giant of 6457 meters. An hour later, we de-boarded in the city Ernesto had dubbed "the Shanghai of America". It was a late Saturday afternoon, just before dusk and we didn't think it an appropriate time to bother the people addressed in all our letters of recommendation. We took our leave of our friend Nogués and went in search of the cheapest lodging we could find. Asking around, we easily found a *pensión* on Yanacocha Street that was a faithful reflection of the price/quality correlation: it was as cheap as it was filthy. For us, it was good enough.

As soon as we got settled, Ernesto wrote with typical sarcasm to his mother:

> Here we are in the fanciest hotel we could find for one day until we decide where to lay our bones. We'll be here for a week at most, so if you haven't written already, don't bother until we get to Lima, which will be in a week or two. The view of La Paz from the train is spectacular—today we'll see what it's like up close.[1]

Completely exhausted, we dragged ourselves to the nearest inn to get something to eat. There was a long table where the locals all sat and were served the plate of the day, a typical Bolivian stew full of mysterious ingredients. Coming from the land of beef and potatoes, we ate it anyway with plenty of hunger but not much conviction. In the back, there were some guitarists to liven up the evening. At one point they played a tango and I felt a lump in my throat—man, was I far from home! I was afraid to even look at Ernesto, but when I finally looked up, I saw that his eyes were all glassy too.

The following day, we bathed as best we could, shaved and ironed our clothes to get ready to go see our potential benefactors in La Paz, armed with all our letters of recommendation. The first stop was the Peñarandas, a well-situated family with relatives in Argentina recommended by our friend Carlos Figueroa's family. They welcomed us with warmth and enthusiasm, just like nearly all the others to follow, inviting us

---

1 William Gálvez Rodríguez, *Viajes y aventuras del joven Ernesto. Ruta del guerrillero,* La Habana, Editorial de Ciencias Sociales, 2002, p. 229.

to eat, showing us around the city and introducing us to people.

The city fascinated us. We loved its colonial architecture, its steep, uneven streets, the Camacho market full of tempting fruits and the lively little bars on 16 de Julio Street. The Church's influence was evident—the city's entire artistic heritage was concentrated in the numerous and fantastic churches. La Paz was flooded with Colla Indians in their colorful clothing, their slow pace and solemn faces so difficult to read. The women carried their infants on their backs. Many were traveling vendors and all appeared to be tired and apathetic about life. They were an unfamiliar race that both surprised and intrigued me. It was funny to see how they shamelessly used the bathroom right in the street. The women, who wore no underclothes, simply just squatted down, took care of business and continued on their way, leaving the steaming product of their bowels behind them. It was an ingrained habit that was hard to change. In many parts of the city, there were notices painted on the walls warning, "Do not urinate. You will be fined." And half of the writing was faded with the urine of people who were impossible to keep in check.

I now understood the impact our indigenous brothers had had on Ernesto during his first trip. But what left the biggest impression on us in La Paz was seeing revolutionary Bolivia in action: the streets were teeming with armed militia groups. That same year a revolutionary movement had led to the election victory of the MNR leaders, Victor Paz Estenssoro and Hernán Siles Zuazo. The revolution aimed at the heart of the Bolivian economic power structure in nationalizing all the tin mines that belonged to the Aramayo, Patiño and Hochschild families. Since tin was the main source of revenue, those families had held absolute economic and political control of the country, while the indigenous majority had lived in miserable poverty and virtual servitude for centuries. The new government had also broken up the Army and announced a significant agrarian reform in the coming days. The country was bubbling with change and there were as many prepared to defend the changes as there were to attack them. The revolution in Bolivia had not, however, come for free. As Ernesto wrote to Tita Infante, "The fight here has been ruthless. Revolutions here are not like in Buenos Aires; two or three thousand dead (no one can say for sure how many) were left lying in the fields."[2] And the fight went on, although by that time both sides were hopeful. One side included the peasants calling for the establishment of the long-awaited agrarian reform and the miners, all members of the Central Obrera Boliviana (COB [Bolivian Workers Party]), which organized marches and armed its members to show their strength to a government they supported, but of which they demanded deeper reforms. The other side constantly talked about the counter-revolution about to happen. The remains of the dissolved Army were restless and there had already been an attempted coups d'etat. And to make matters worse, there were internal divisions within the government. Ernesto described them thus:

> The MNR is a conglomerate consisting of three more or less notable leanings: the right, represented by Siles Zuazo, Vice President and hero of the revolution; the center, represented by Paz Estenssoro, a bit more slippery, but probably just as rightwing as the first; and the left, represented by Lechin, who is

2 Adys Cupull and Froilán González, *Cálida presencia. La amistad del "Che" y Tita Infante a través de sus cartas*, Rosario, Ameghino, 1997, p. 44.

Isaías Nougués and his son, José María, two of the people who helped us most in Bolivia. Ernesto describes Don Isaías as follows: "His political ideas are old-fashioned anywhere in the world, but he sticks to them regardless of the proletariat hurricane unleashed all over our warmongering planet. His friendly hand extends to any Argentine without question, and his august serenity blankets us miserable mortals in eternal, fatherly protection."

the clear leader of a movement for serious change, but who I personally believe is a carousing, womanizing upstart. Power will most likely end up firmly in Lechin's group, since he has the support of the armed miners; however, the resistance offered by his government colleagues may be significant, especially now that the Army is being regrouped.[3]

The analysis was written at the end of our stay in Bolivia—which ended up lasting more than a month instead of a week—and shows Ernesto's political maturity and what mattered to him in his travels, which went

---

3 Ib., p. 44 and 45.

way beyond standard tourism. Of course, we couldn't perceive these subtleties at first and were simply surprised by the shots that rang out all over the city, the slogans painted on the walls and the indigenous men that appeared to have taken over the country. "A rich variety of adventurers of all nationalities grows and flourishes within the multi-colored, mestizo masses of the city, leading the country toward its destiny;"[4] this was the first impression that Ernesto recorded in his journal that Sunday that we began to explore the city.

A few days later, we were having coffee in a café in La Paz and we saw firsthand the humiliation the Indians suffered in Bolivia. A woman was enjoying afternoon tea with her children, while the children's nanny sat on the floor and they threw their scraps down for her to eat as if she were a dog. We couldn't believe we were seeing this in the twentieth century. It was then that José María Nougués, the fellow we had met on the train, showed up as were looking on in horror and talking about this scenario. Once again, fate was on our side. He introduced us to his father, Isaías Nougués, a very important man in the Argentine community that had settled in Bolivia. He had been governor of Tucumán Province and founder of the Blanco Party, but his anti-Peronism had led him into exile. He liked us immediately. Isaías knew our parents, even our mothers, complimenting them and saying that they were both very pretty. He simply adopted us and left the doors to his home open wide to us. The Nougués' magnificent house was on the outskirts of La Paz in the Calacoto area. It was a place where both civil and military exiles of Peronism gathered, as well as much of La Paz society. Nougués was even a friend of the President, Estenssoro. So we were able to rub elbows at the numerous

---

4 E. Guevara, *Otra vez*, p. 12.

barbeques and dinners we were invited to with the people who were in the social and political spotlight at that time. Señor Nougués was quite a character, like an old political boss with a halo of gentility—a "nobleman from Tucumán" in Ernesto's words. He describes him in his journal:

> His political ideas are old-fashioned anywhere in the world, but he sticks to them regardless of the proletariat hurricane unleashed all over our warmongering planet. His friendly hand extends to any Argentine without question, and his august serenity blankets us miserable mortals in eternal, fatherly protection.[5]

That protection led us to live out extreme contrasts during our stay in Bolivia. We attended both the gatherings, parties and meeting places of the La Paz high society, but we also mixed with ordinary people and had significant experiences like the visit to the Bolsa Negra mine.

One of the key places we got to know thanks to Nougués was the Gallo de Oro Tavern where political issues were brewed; many even joked that is was the second house of government. Between wine and women, the leaders of the revolution mixed with land- and mine-owners, as well as Argentine exiles and adventurers. It was a well-hidden, exclusive place on the outskirts of the city—you could only get there by escort with one of the "regulars". The Nouguéses took us by car, which was pretty dangerous since we had to get through a roadblock of armed campesinos. One day, as we were coming back from El Gallo in the car with Gogo, Nougués' brother, an indigenous patrol stopped us at gunpoint. I thought they were going to shoot us on the spot. One of them came up and asked for documentation. Gogo, who

---

5 Ib., p. 14.

was pretty drunk and had that easygoing way of the master of the plantation, said to him, "*Che*, put that gun away and save it for the pheasants." We got away with it—they let us go. Ernesto and I were pretty oblivious to the danger, despite the fact that we knew there were deaths every night as a result of this type of encounter.

We sat at a table in the Gallo de Oro with important men who discussed political matters and, since we were younger and disagreed with many of the comments rooted in the privileged social position enjoyed by these men, we listened more than talked. Like always, Ernesto captured this elite way of thinking in a paragraph:

> The so-called well-to-do, refined people are surprised by what's happening and malign the importance given to the Indians and mestizos, but I've noticed a spark of nationalist enthusiasm in all of them for some of what the government's doing. No one denies the need for the government to do away with everything that symbolizes the power of the three mining families, and the young people think this is a step forward in the struggle towards equality among people and fortunes.[6]

But not all was political at the Gallo. There were all sorts of dilettantes, fortune-seekers and playboys as well. Gogo was one of them—an authentic dandy, who entertained between whiskies with stories of his stints in Europe among friends the likes of Aristotle Onassis. Of course, he always paid for our drinks. And there wasn't just liquor going around there. One night, Ernesto came back from the bathroom all intrigued and whispered to me that he had seen some guys who had been at the

---

6 Ib., p. 12.

Here we are saying goodbye to José María Nougués at the train station outside La Paz. We each took the photo that the other appears in. Nougués was returning to Buenos Aires after his visit with his father. I don't recall the names of the couple in the photos.

table with us sniffing something from a pouch.

"That's cocaine, you idiot—we're in Bolivia," I told him self-assuredly; I had a young uncle, Quique Ferrer, who had shown me the "real" nightlife in Buenos Aires. He had taken my friends and me to the cabarets and tango joints. In 1950s Buenos Aires, drugs were already around; but Ernesto was completely unaware of their existence. When we told the Nouguéses, they split their sides laughing, "Yeah, this is where you get the finest coke in the world!" Cocaine was so readily available in La Paz that you could buy bags of it, not little packets or "raviolis" as we called them in Buenos Aires, and they offered them to you everywhere.

The first advantage we got from knowing the Nougueses was improved accommodations. The very first day we met, Isaías got us a much better place for the same price through his contacts. The hotel was modest, but clean. We would grab something to eat and then go to have coffee with Nougués and his friends who had just finished their lunch at the Hotel Sucre, the most exclusive in La Paz. One day, there were some leftovers and we asked if they were going to finish them; from then on, the waiters, who liked us, saved everything the others had left uneaten for when we arrived for "coffee". And we were forever grateful, because our chastity belt was becoming thinner by the minute and we still had a long journey ahead. We ate so much that Gogo Nougués told us that in Lima, where we were planning to meet up with him, he was going to take us to a restaurant that would give anyone who ate more than three chickens their meal for free.

"I'm going to take you as the Argentine 'exhibit', because you eat everything and still look like sticks," he laughed. We went to the hotel so often that one of Ernesto's letters to his mothers is written on Sucre Palace Hotel stationary ("...check out the epigraph," he jokes in reference to the letterhead). Since I was more a friend of the "good life" than Ernesto, I was thrilled with our new acquaintances. In one of my letters to my mother, dated July 22, I write:

> The good families in La Paz invite us out to eat, they show us around by car and we've been invited to a party. We went to a tavern, the Gallo de Oro, that belongs to an Argentine. They don't let us pay for

anything. All the Argentines here are really close-knit and have treated us fantastically well. There's always an afternoon tea to attend, meals in the Sucre and the Hotel La Paz, the two best hotels … This afternoon we're going to have tea with a couple of pretty girls and tonight we're going to a dance.

I dragged Ernesto along, trying to get him to dress a little better, because he was ever-faithful to his custom of wearing just anything, even if the party was at an embassy or a swanky house. In spite of the parties, all the food and all the nights on the town, things were still smooth-sailing with Ernesto's asthma. He tromped up and down the streets with that typical Guevara gait and often I was the one being dragged along, since I got tired easily or the altitude got to me. One day, Nougués ran into him by chance while he was waiting in line to eat some stew at a street stall and he asked him how he could just eat anything like that.

"It's just that I've spent my whole life being careful with food because of my asthma; so now that I feel good, I don't want to pass up any opportunity to try something new," Ernesto responded.

Our visits to the Hotel Sucre were not only to social-ize and eat—the hotel terrace was the best balcony for watching the miners' marches down the main street. They would parade by, shooting into the air with their machine guns. They were powerful demonstrations of force in the face of the oligarchy. Ernesto's critical eye left his impressions in his journal:

They paraded by in an endless procession of unions, professional associations and syndicates all firing off their Mausers assiduously. Every few paces, one of the different group leaders would yell,

'*Compañeros* of Union X, *viva* La Paz, *viva* American independence, *viva* Bolivia; glory to the protomartyrs of independence, glory to Pedro Domingo Murillo, glory to Guzmán, glory to Villarroel'. The recitation was uttered in a tired voice to a chorus of other monotonous voices dutifully echoing it. It was a picturesque demonstration that lacked vigor. The trudging pace and lack of enthusiasm by all robbed it of vitality; those in the know said that it was missing the energetic faces of the miners.[7]

Our first excursion outside the city was to the *yungas*, a fertile valley close to the jungle you get to after crossing the mountains that surround the city and that, to us, was like an explosion of green after so much arid land. We hitched a ride on a truck, took the road all the way up to a ridge more than 4500 meters high called La Cumbre and then began our descent down into the valley. Ernesto describes the landscape thus:

> On either lush side going down to the river hundreds of meters below, blanketed under a cloud-filled sky, the coconut groves were scattered between the typical tiers of banana trees that, from a distance, looked like green propellers emerging from the jungle of orange and other citrus trees, of coffee trees red with berries; all of this was highlighted by the scant figure of a parrot that somewhat resembled a flame and other fruit and tropical trees.[8]

We spent two basically touristy, enjoyable days there, although we were really beginning to feel the lack of

---

7 Ib., p. 12 and 13.
8 Ib., p. 13.

Ernesto with Nougués and other friends in the train station in La Paz in a photo I took. We had gone to meet Isaías Nougués' brother, Gogo, a playboy with whom spent many nights out in La Paz. Ernesto is in the lower part of the photo beside José María Nougués and another Argentine called Paso. Above, from left to right, Gogo, a couple whose name I don't recall, Manolo Reyna, Isaías Nougués and Lucas, also Argentine.

female presence that had accompanied us since our departure from Buenos Aires. Ernesto shared the sentiment: "We spent two fantastic days in the yungas, but we needed two women to add a touch of the erotic to all that greenery around us."[9]

But we would have to make do for the moment with just the lush vegetation. We visited a Salesian farm/school where the brothers educated the local Indians. The German priest that greeted us very kindly showed us around, but even though everything appeared to be as it should, Ernesto, always with his sights set a bit higher, later reflected, "The Indian is still seen as a savage by white men, particularly Europeans, for as many robes as they

---

[9] Ib., p. 13.

might wear."[10] We returned to La Paz in the pick-up of some guys we had met there.

When we got back, I decided to rectify as soon as possible the female drought that afflicted us. While watching one of the numerous protest marches from the Hotel Sucre terrace, I saw two beautiful girls in the crowd. Without thinking twice about it, I went down and approached them to strike up a conversation or "hook up", as we used to say. Being an Argentine, it was always easy to get girls to talk—they saw you as someone special, interesting—so we began to chat.

Just then a short, dark guy in his thirties joined the conversation and immediately suggested the four of us go for drinks. I started to get nervous, because I didn't have a dime in my pocket and proposed we leave it for the following day. He insisted and the girls agreed instantly, so I was left with no choice but to join them. I signaled to Ernesto, who was still on the hotel terrace, that we were going. Once in the bar, I ordered a lowly coffee, but the others began to order pastries, sandwiches —the guy even ordered an imported whisky. I was thinking to myself, Today, I wash dishes. The conversation became livelier and everything on the romantic front was going well, but when the guy called the waiter over to order another round, I began to make signals so he'd get the message that I was completely broke.

"Don't worry, man—I'm paying," he said in a burst of laughter. And the hook-up was a complete success—we each ended up with one of the girls.

Once the girls were gone, my new friend explained his situation. His name was Ramírez and he was a Venezuelan Colonel who, as punishment for an attempt to overthrow the dictator, Pérez Jiménez, had been rele-

---

10 Ib., p. 13 and 14.

gated to the Venezualan Consulate in Bolivia as a military attaché. With a salary paid in Venezualan bolivars, he lived like a king in La Paz. Assiduous parishioner of the Gallo de Oro and the Hotel Sucre, he promptly became one of us. Besides, our respective romances continued with the two girls we had met that day. Ernesto, on the other hand, had also met a girl at a party, Martha Pinilla, the daughter of a rich, aristocratic family that owned lots of land and properties outside the city. "Something curvy with a bust has crossed my path, so we'll see...,"[11] Ernesto describes her in his journal. As far as women were concerned, we were just about set.

While we spent our days in the Bolivian capital in a sort of schizophrenic back-and-forth between high-society life and discovering the emerging social reality, very far away from La Paz, an event was occurring that would mark Ernesto for life. In the early morning of July 26, 1953, while we were surely sleeping off some party, the first revolutionary action was under way in Cuba under the command of the young, then unknown Fidel Castro. They attacked the Moncada military headquarters in Santiago de Cuba intending to overthrow the military dictator, Fulgencio Batista. The attack was unsuccessful and there was a military reprisal which left 70 rebels dead. The survivors, which included Fidel Castro, then 26, and his brother Raúl, were jailed.

We got the news a few days later in the Nougués' house, but many of us were doubtful, since the reports were issued exclusively by the Cuban government. We thought it was just one more revolt against one of the many dictatorships that ruled our America. Ernesto had no idea where destiny would lead him, but he was aware that he was headed towards something. I think this is why he

---

11 Ib., p. 14.

wrote obsessively about everything he experienced on that trip—he had a premonition that something important was going to happen. "We're going to end up getting mixed up in some little war," he told me half joking, half serious.

Two issues remained unresolved and worried us: our finances, which were rapidly depleting despite the favorable exchange rate and the generosity of our new friends; and the visas that would allow us to continue our journey or not. The visa for Ecuador we got easily enough through the numerous contacts of the Nouguéses. But the main problem continued to be Venezuela, nearly impossible to obtain. My providential encounter with Colonel Ramírez had to be good for something other than just the romance he had gotten me mixed up in. So one day over lunch, I told him about our problem and what had happened at our failed attempt with the consul in Buenos Aires.

"That guy is a son-of-a-bitch," Ramírez told me. Two days later he brought Ernesto and me our visas.

"See how I stepped on his fat belly after all?" Ernesto said with a triumphant smile.

We had yet to resolve our economic situation, which grew worse by the minute. Ernesto dusted off one of the letters of recommendation—the one from Dr. Ferreira in Buenos Aires to the Bolivian School of Medicine. So there we went and met a Dr. Molina who treated us very kindly, offering Ernesto three months' work as a doctor in a mine and me as a nurse. We accepted, but only for one month, because we were afraid of spending all the money and ending up trapped indefinitely in Bolivia.

The salary in Bolivian currency was worth practically nothing in the rest of Latin America. We returned to our hotel, enthusiastically having promised to meet him again the following day to organize the details. Everything

"It's a powerful sight: Behind, the august Illimani, serene and majestic; in front, the white Mururata sprinkled with the mining buildings that look like flakes of some kind scattered along the slopes of the peak and held in place at the whim of the terrain. An enormous gamma of dark tones sparkle on the mountain, the silence of the still mine striking even those like us who don't know its language." This is how Ernesto described the landscape on the way to the Bolsa Negra mine. He also took the photos.

was falling into place: We had the visas and a job to recover some of the money we had spent and that also interested us in that it offered us the chance to live and work with the miners for a whole month and see their reality from up close. And as an added bonus, our love interests were sailing along nicely. The Pinilla girl was about 22 or 23, taller than Ernesto, both pretty and distinguished, the daughter of a Bolivian diplomat; she spoke correct English, having studied in New York and Washington. She and her family were opposed to the revolutionary movement, but kept quiet about it, since the diplomatic corps had been barely touched by the new government. Ernesto really liked her, even though they argued over politics. That night we went out like most nights with both girls and toasted all our good news.

The next morning, we got out Ernesto's "Jorge" suit again and my pinstripe (the one my mother had saved after that ill-fated last night in Buenos Aires), and headed out in our finest for the medical school again. To our surprise, a very nice young woman informed us that Dr. Molina had gone out for two or three days to do inspections at the mines. Not giving up, we returned three days later, and this time the young woman asked us to come back "in a couple of days". And that was how it went for nearly three weeks, coming and going like some comedy of errors, our suits more and more wrinkled, our chastity belt thinner and thinner, not to mention our hopes. When the doctor finally returned, we decided not to accept the job, because all the waiting plus the extra month of work would have meant a stay of nearly two months in Bolivia, something our finances would not allow. It was a difficult decision, because we were interested in the socio-political situation going on at that moment in Bolivia and wanted to stay and witness it up close, particularly since there had been rumors of an imminent people's uprising, which in the end, didn't occur. But on the other hand, it was clear to us that the final objective of our trip was to get to Venezuela. We were at least able to get Dr. Molina to give us a letter of recommendation to visit a wolfram mine in the mountains.

Thanks to that recommendation, we had lodging secured at the mine; however, we didn't have a ticket to get there or money to buy it. So Ernesto dug into his experience from the last trip and we went to a nearby market to ask who was going in that direction. A trucker agreed to give us a lift and we left early the next morning. Fortunately, the trucker was traveling alone and let us ride in the cabin with him, because it was deathly cold out and getting colder the higher we ascended the frosty slopes of the Illimani. Every so often, we'd pass a truck carrying Indians in the flatbed; they were absolutely unperturbed by the cold. Our truck was a real wreck and the steep grades up and down had us worried about the brakes.

"Don't worry, don't worry," the driver tried to put us at ease as he drove along as if on a peaceful Sunday drive in the park. Every once in while, we'd reach a plateau where the road would flatten out and allow us to catch our breath. It was on one of these breathers that Ernesto remembered that Martha had told him her family had a ranch in this area that the government was about to expropriate.

"Where does the Pinilla ranch property begin?" he asked the driver.

"A ways back."

"And where does it end?"

"Long way to go yet."

"*Che*, how about that rich girl you snagged," I kidded him, "she owns half of Bolivia."

As the hours passed, every time we asked the driver if the Pinilla property had ended, he always said, "Not yet." Finally, after hours of driving, he stopped the truck and said, "This is where it ends." We got out to stretch our legs and take a look around. There was a stand by a couple of shacks in a frighteningly miserable state. We chatted with the Indians who worked for the Pinillas and they told us some really sad stories that made us feel awful. They said they were only allowed to eat the corn that grew in the area, but couldn't keep animals, not even a hen for eggs or a cow for milk.

We continued our ascent all the way to 5000 meters and began the descent down into the valley where the Bolsa Negra mining offices lay. The landscape was stunning. Ernesto describes it eloquently:

> It's a powerful sight: Behind, the august Illimani, serene and majestic; in front, the white Mururata sprinkled with the mining buildings that look like flakes of some kind scattered along the slopes of the peak and held in place at the whim of the terrain. An enormous gamma of dark tones sparkle on the mountain, the silence of the still mine striking even those like us who don't know its language.[12]

It was nearly nightfall and, after having traveled all day, we were exhausted. The engineers welcomed us warmly, fed us dinner, we exchanged a few anecdotes and then we went to bed.

The following morning was a Sunday and we awoke to snow-covered mountains. With one of the engineers as our guide, we went to see a glacier-fed lake on the Mururata peak and then he showed us a mill for grinding

---

12 Ib., p. 14.

Ernesto photographed me at the Bolsa Negra mine with the engineer and the manager. Both served as guides and explained the entire functioning of the wolfram mine, which had just been nationalized. The place was deserted, because all the miners had gone to La Paz to participate in a rally. "But the mine felt still. It lacked the thrust of the arms that tear the load of material from the earth every day," described Ernesto.

the mineral the miners extracted from the shaft to obtain the wolfram. They gave us all sorts of interesting technical explanations that Ernesto diligently jotted down to later transfer to his journal. We were anxious to see inside the shaft, to get into the deep recesses of the mountain, but it had gotten late, so we left it for the next day.

We set out very early for the mountain where the vein they were extracting from lay. They dressed us in rain slickers and rubber boots and gave us carbon lamps. Entering the mine was an experience in itself, but what left its impression upon both of us most was what we saw when we came back to the surface. A few meters from the mine exit, there was a shantytown where the miners lived with their families, and the engineers pointed out the machine guns strategically placed aiming at the shacks. At that point the government had already nationalized the mine and it fell under the auspices of the Secretary of Mining Affairs, but until just recently, when it was still privately owned by the grand feudal families of Bolivia, the guns were often fired at the miners and their families as punishment for having asked for a raise or improved working conditions. They told us that these machine guns had wiped out everything in their path, even the bugs. Now things had changed and the miners not only had acquired social and labor rights, they had also been armed by the government as a people's militia. In fact, while we were visiting the mine, the workers were in La Paz at a rally in support of the government and the agrarian reform, celebrating Aug. 2, the Day of the Indian and because there were rumors of counter-revolution. Everything seemed even sadder and more silent without the presence of the miners, as Ernesto noted in his journal: "But the mine felt still. It lacked the thrust of the arms that tear the load of material from the earth every day."[13]

That afternoon, the miners returned in a convoy of several trucks. We saw them approach from far off between the mountains, firing their rifles and machine guns into the air. The shots were multiplied by their echoes and Ernesto and I were rendered silent by that poetic image of the power of the people, thinking that those same men that seemed so invincible and powerful that day had not long ago been at the mercy of the guns pointed at their homes.

"The miners arrived with their stony faces and colored plastic helmets that made them seem like warriors from some other land,"[14] noted Ernesto. We saw them

---

13 Ib., p. 15.
14 Ib., p. 15.

get out of the trucks and turn their arms in at the warehouse. They all looked to be about 50 or 60 years old, but they were actually not older than 30. They were almost all afflicted with lung diseases, having worked themselves to the bone all their lives without protection, without proper hours. The only medical attention they had was from a medic who lived at the mine. Ernesto was interested in the sanitary conditions, particularly in the case of births. The miners, just like the Indians, did not allow anyone to be involved in delivering babies—births were handled by their own midwives.

We took advantage of the chance to get a ride back to La Paz on one of the trucks headed that way.

The days spent in the mine had given us a deeper understanding of the social movement afoot in Bolivia and increased our interest in that country of so many stark contrasts. However, our decision to continue traveling had already been made; we had our visas and very little money left. It was around that time that Ernesto wrote to his father:

> I'm a bit disappointed that we're not staying longer, because this is a truly fascinating country going through a particularly effervescent moment ... We've seen incredible marches of people armed with Mausers and tossing stuff just for the hell of it. You hear shots fired every day and there are injuries and deaths from shootings ... Human life is given little importance here—it's granted or taken away without much ado; however interesting this situation may be for neutral observers like us, all seek some pretext or other to find the quickest exit, us included.[15]

---

15 E. Guevara Lynch, ...Aquí va un soldado de América, p. 15.

Ernesto, despite his admiration for many aspects of the revolution taking place in Bolivia, never lost his critical eye or his sense of humor. He sarcastically called it the "DDT revolution", commenting on it in a letter to his father about the Bolivian authorities: "The government has proved nearly incapable of stopping or even channeling the miners and peasant masses, but the latter do respond to a certain degree and I've no doubt that if there were an armed revolt by the opposition, they'd side with the MNR."[16] Ernesto invented the "DDT" nickname after our visit to the Ministry of Indian Affairs. He managed to get us an interview with the minister, Ñuflo Chávez, an Indian with a law degree who spoke both Quechua and Aimará. He heard out the dramas suffered by the indigenous delegations who came to voice their woes in his very sumptuous offices decked out with curtains, rugs and upholstered furniture. Since they assumed all Indians had head lice, he had them all sprinkled with DDT powder—faces, necks, shirt collars and hair—before entering his office. You would often see Indians out in the city with their eyebrows, lashes and hair covered with white dust. "Look at that," Ernesto and I joked with each other, "he must have been to see Chávez." The Minister kindly received us and gave us several books on the Bolivian revolutionary movement.

As we became more and more immersed in Bolivian politics, we also gained confidence to participate in the discussions in the Gallo de Oro or in the Nougués house, particularly Ernesto who, in addition to his formal education, had the experience of all the Guevara dinner-table debates. Ernesto had long conversations with all types of characters and confidently defended his posi-

---

16 Ib., p. 15.

"The miners arrived with their stony faces and colored plastic helmets that made them seem like warriors from some other land," wrote Ernesto, moved by that poetic image of the power of the people. He took this picture of me with the mine workers the day they returned from participating in a support rally for the new revolutionary government in La Paz. One of the first measures passed by the MNR had been the break-up of the Army and the establishment of people's militias.

tion. He supported the revolution in Bolivia for its achievements, but deep-down he wanted even more, because he sought perfection and was unwavering in his convictions. He couldn't accept sins like accepting the fringe benefits and gifts that come with positions of power. By then, he was already firm in his conviction that the worst of all political evils was Yankee imperialism. Among the high society ranks in which we moved in La Paz, many were scandalized by his opinions and critical of the revolutionary government.

"They're not like us. Imagine the country in the hands of Indians," they'd say and clearly thought the country belonged to them, the upper crust. The closest example we had was the family of Ernesto's girlfriend, the Pinillas, who were about to have that enormous tract of land we crossed on our way to the mine expropriated.

"Now I understand why your family is so opposed to the government," Ernesto joked with her.

The Nouguéses, even though they held an opinion different from ours, were open-minded and understanding people with whom you could talk about anything. One of the people we met at their house was Ricardo Rojo (El Gordo), a 35-yr-old Argentine lawyer and leading member of Radical Party who had had to flee Argentina for having defended political prisoners during Peronism. He had himself been jailed prior to exile by two hard-core Peronist commissaries. He then was able to pull off a movie-like escape and took refuge in the Guatemalan Embassy. The ambassador personally escorted him to the airport and put him on a plane for La Paz, where we would later meet him.

The story of his escape was even published in Life Magazine and, for two young adventurers like us, was impressive, needless to say. Ernesto wrote, in a letter to his father: "In Bolivia we met a Radical leader who pulled an incredible *piante*[17] from a commissary about four months ago. We later saw him in Perú and also ran into him in Guayaquil."[18] Rojo was "stationed" for the moment in Bolivia, seeing where he'd head next and gladly joined our nomadic existence in La Paz. However, as can be seen in Ernesto's letter, he didn't accompany us on our journey as sustained in his book.[19]

Many other Argentines passed through the Nougués house, mostly hustlers. We met many who came looking to find gold in the Beni, an area of Bolivia close to a river

---

17 Escape.
18 E. Guevara Lynch, *...Aquí va un soldado de América*, p. 25.
19 Ricardo Rojo, *Mi amigo el Che*, Buenos Aires, Sudamericana, 1996.

where gold had been discovered. Most were more broke than they had been when they arrived, having *patinado*[20] what little gold they found on women, alcohol and gambling, and now didn't even have a return ticket to their names. They were adventurers like us, although we weren't looking to get rich, but rather to gain knowledge and live out new experiences. They had spectacular stories and gave us valuable advice for our trip. It seems that the hustlers were more dangerous than snakes and crocodiles—there were some serious mafias. So they told us, "When you guys are out there on the road and you feel the need to relieve yourselves, sit one in front of the other to cover each other's back." It was good advice that we always followed; no matter what hour it was, whenever nature called, we woke the other to stand guard.

Everyday one of us took the initiative and said, "OK, let's get out of here once and for all," and the other would convince him, "No, just a little bit longer." We certainly weren't lacking reasons to stay. Bolivia was a nice place, we enjoyed all the amenities, everything was close by and what was going on socially and politically interested us. Ernesto had already formed a very clear idea of the social drama being played out in Latin America, the tragedy of poverty, the gulf that separated those who had everything from those who had nothing, the lack of healthcare and education. Our experiences in Bolivia shaped his ideas even further. There, the injustice was tangible and one could also see the latent power in an awakening populace.

We finally made the decision to go; we had spent half of our reserves from the chastity belt. "Everything was finally ready for our departure, each with his own love interest to leave behind. My farewell was more on the

---

20 Spent.

intellectual side with no sweetness, but I do think there's something between us, she and I,"[21] Ernesto confessed in his journal. It was hard for us both to leave; the experience in La Paz had been intense and our respective romances had meant more than we had expected. In a moment of desperation, I even proposed to Ernesto that I should bring my girlfriend along with us. He, always the more level-headed, smacked me to my senses. To his mother he sarcastically wrote, "Considering everything, it wouldn't be so strange for you to have a Bolivian grandchild in addition to your little girls."[22] Our biggest concern prior to leaving was how to earn a few pesos. We found the solution in one of the oldest tricks in the world: gambling. Thanks to a poker game, we earned some "dirty pesos"[23], according to Ernesto's confession in a letter to Celia that he sent via a friend who was traveling to Argentina, along with the ashtray he bought with the earnings.

We set a date for departure and decided on our next steps. Before entering Perú, we wanted to see Lake Titicaca, which was on the border between the two countries and hid an archaeological treasure on one of its islands. The Nouguéses kept telling us, "No, don't go; stay a little longer;" they enjoyed our company, because there was always something to talk about or a joke for a good laugh. But since our departure was inevitable, we consoled ourselves promising to meet up with Gogo Nougués in Lima, where he planned to travel, of course by plane like a rich boy. We also arranged to meet Rojo in Perú, but he'd travel alone. The farewell party was a big to-do at the Nougués' house. Our girls were there, along with our friends and acquaintances. The libations

21 E. Guevara, *Otra vez*, p. 16.
22 W. Gálvez Rodríguez, Op. cit., p. 236.
23 Ib., p. 235.

This photo has particular sentimental value for me since it was the last one taken of the two of us together (one of us was always behind the camera while the other posed). The photo was taken in Bolivia where, 14 years later, Ernesto was shot. We were on the outskirts of La Paz on a Sunday stroll with the Peñaranda family. This family was one of those that helped us out thanks to the letters of recommendation we had brought. This contact had come through Carlos Figueroa's family. As was customary back then, even on a "low-budget" trip like ours, outings with high-society people were jacket-and-tie affairs.

were significant, as Ernesto attests to in his journal.

We had arranged a ride with a trucker who would take us as far as Bahía de Copacabana the following day. As could be expected, we overslept and had to make a run for it, dragging all our stuff behind, so as not to miss our ride.

It was a slow, picturesque trip over mountain roads that didn't allow for speed, with stops in every little town to pick up chickens, calves, packages, etc. We traveled in the cab for a while, then would switch to the back to watch the scenery. We stood out everywhere as the only white men in a completely indigenous population. When we were about half-way there, Ernesto realized he had forgotten the camera in our rush to leave.

"I'm going back to get it. We'll meet up in Copacabana," he said decisively.

"You're crazy—let someone who's coming to Lima bring it."

"No, I'm going. You take the luggage and wait for me there. I bet I get there before you," he joked. He was like that—there was no convincing him otherwise. For Ernesto, the camera was sacred. Right then and there, he got out of the truck and started hitching in the other direction. I consoled myself in the knowledge that at least it would be easy to find each other in the town since, as I said, we really stood out.

So I arrived alone in Bahía de Copacabana, a spectacular place on the banks of Lake Titicaca. It is the highest lake in the world at 4000 meters above sea level. It is vast and has two islands in the middle, the Isla del Sol and the Isla de la Luna, the latter belonging to the military—I believe there was a prison there. The Isla del Sol, however, held a temple that we wanted to see.

I got off the truck with an impossible load of suitcases, but managed to get to a pensión thanks to the little group of Indians always at the ready to help out in exchange for a few coins. My biggest concern was finding somewhere to stay that was safe to leave our belongings. Once I got settled, I went out for a walk to take in the scenery, which was spectacular—a silent, sad place under a translucent sky, pleasant in the daytime and cold at night. On the edge of the lake, there was a good hotel where the North American tourists stayed. I was wearing my famous López Taibo boots, a suede jacket and bandana on my neck—in other words, I looked good. Perhaps that was why, or perhaps just out of curiosity, a woman approached me and asked, "Are you Argentine?"

"Yes, I am," I answered, surprised to hear that she also had an Argentinean accent.

"And what are you doing here?"

"I'm waiting for a friend who's a doctor. We're traveling through Latin America, learning about the fight against leprosy and doing a bit of tourism along the way."

The woman did turn out to be Argentine and she was the manager of the tourist hotel. She invited me to have coffee in the café there and it wasn't long before she invited us to stay for free in the hotel. I declined at first—just enough—and then finally accepted. She talked me into it by saying that it was low season, there were hardly any guests and she didn't have anyone to talk to; she was happy to have fellow Argentines around. She told me her story, which was not a happy one. She was a single mother with a child with behavioral problems, so she had gone to live in that remote place to raise him far from everything.

When Ernesto finally arrived, I greeted him with the good news, "*Chancho*! Guess where we're staying—see that 5-star hotel there on the edge of the lake? Right there! I got it—"

"You idiot! It must have cost a fortune! I told you we were through with the high-class stuff when we left La Paz—we'll end up broke now—! "

"—for free. It's not costing us a cent and we even get the food included. You can thank my good looks and my boots that you so like to criticize."

Once we were settled in our fancy rooms, we began to plan our excursion to the Isla del Sol that Ernesto had been dreaming about since we left Buenos Aires. He had read extensively on Inca culture and knew where the most significant vestiges of that civilization were. Through our friend in the hotel, we were able to hire a local to take us by canoe to the island and be our guide. We set out at five in the morning with a picnic basket prepared by the hotel. The canoe was quite large and had oars as well as a sail. The trip to the island went smoothly without incident, although there wasn't much wind, so we had to row. Once on the island by around 11 a.m., two or three Indians greeted us and showed us around some ruins that were close to the shore, explaining that they were the Templo del Sol. It may have been easy to get away with it with the North American tourists, but Ernesto knew better and couldn't be fooled so easily.

"This isn't the Templo del Sol," he retorted. They swore that those were the only ruins on the island. Things began to get tense and the argument to get louder. I was estimating the strength of the men and, even though I realized we'd win hands down in a fist-fight, I was afraid they might be armed or that there might be more of them. Finally, the Indian from the boat broke ranks and admitted that the Templo del Sol was in the middle of the island, but he warned that it was a two-hour walk and that would make it too late to make the journey back.

"Doesn't matter—let's go," said Ernesto. So we made the hike across the island, which had a landscape much like that of the altiplano, but with more vegetation due to its proximity to water. When we got to the temple, we discovered that it was completely destroyed, a ruin of ruins, everything looted. Ernesto, having read so much on the place, explained, "This is where the highest-ranking Inca sat" and "this is where they made ritual sacrifices." It was a magical moment—the view of the lake from so high up was spectacular and even more so because it was accentuated by all the history surrounding us. Ernesto went through the ruins, searching for something that he finally found: a small Inca statue, "an idol representing a woman that practically fulfils all my aspirations."[24] The Indian shook us out of our enchantment

---

24 E. Guevara, *Otra vez*, p. 17.

Photo taken by Ernesto. We were on Lake Titicaca on a canoe headed for the Isla del Sol where we hoped to see the Incan Templo del Sol. Next to me, the owner of the boat. The sun was still shining and our troubles had not yet begun. We had to row due to the lack of wind.

telling us to hurry because it was getting late and starting to get dark.

We started the hike back and by the time we reached the shore where the boat was, it was already night and the driver didn't want to set sail, saying it was too dangerous.

Faced with the prospect of spending the night on that inhospitable island, we talked him into sailing nevertheless. The canoe was wide and easy to sail, but after about half an hour, a wicked storm brewed up and we began to spin like a cocktail mixer. The Indian gave up in desperation, dropped the oars, threw himself on the deck of the canoe and started praying. First he prayed to Pachamama[25], then he recited the Lord's Prayer and the

---

25 Incan goddess of the earth.

Ave María—he prayed to them all, just in case. We had to take over our perilous situation, so we grabbed the oars and gave it all we had. We took turns because our hands were bleeding. At one point, I was sure we were going to flip over any minute and I started to take my boots off.

Ernesto, without breaking his stride, asked me, "What are you taking your boots off for?"

"Well … any minute now, we're gonna end up in the water and have to swim for it."

"Don't be an idiot. If you fall in the water, you'll be dead in five minutes from freezing," he said, completely calm and logical.

I put my boots back on, thinking that this was the end. There we were at night 4000 meters above sea-level in the middle of a giant, freezing-cold lake that looked more like an ocean because of all the waves whipped up by the storm. We pushed onward and kept rowing; after a while, we saw some tiny lights in the distance and tried to head towards them. Finally, we were able to bring the boat into a bay. You could hear dogs barking far off and some Indians appeared with lanterns to bring us in to shore. The atmosphere was not the best; they were angry at us for having risked the boatman's life and for having stuck our noses in the tourist routine. In addition, that land was a private ranch and we were not entitled to dock the boat there. Nevertheless, the head Indian gave us permission to spend the night in a barn until the storm passed. Ernesto and I checked the place over and made sure the door opened to the inside; we laid down with our feet facing the door to stop anyone who tried to open it. We knew that we were sitting ducks if anyone wanted to do us harm—they outnumbered us by dozens. We fell asleep in spite of the danger and the straw we were sleeping on. Before falling asleep, it occurred to me that the unbelievable calm of my friend in the face of such adversity was what had saved us. He had it clear in his mind that our only resort was to row like hell and not waste time on silly speculations like mine. He had a gift for accepting reality for what it was and doing what was necessary to make the best of it.

The following morning we awoke to the sun on our faces, chickens crawling over our legs and the Indians who barely managed not to step on us as they went about getting their work tools. We thought we had been so clever, but we hadn't realized that the doors also opened to the outside ...

We set sail again in the canoe in route to Bahía de Copacabana. This time we let the Indian do the rowing, because we were exhausted from the effort of the previous day—"we couldn't move a muscle because of the paralyzing exhaustion,"[26] Ernesto admitted in his journal. Our friend at the hotel was relieved to see us—she thought we had drowned in the lake during the storm and was about to send out a search party. We slept more than a few hours to recover and get ready to travel, since we planned to leave the next day for Puno on the Peruvian border.

In the afternoon we went out for a walk in the village and decided to visit the church there, famous for its Virgin of Copacabana and other important relics. There was a blind man at the door playing sad altiplano music with a one-string violin to a congregation of lepers, beggars and the diseased—it was a place of pilgrimage for all kinds. When we entered to see inside the church, we came upon the most amazing scene of our whole trip: A fat priest dressed in his cassock, with bills stuck between his fingers as if he were directing a game of craps, received one by one the Indians waiting in an

---

26 E. Guevara, *Otra vez*, p. 17.

endless line for his blessing. The priest would utter a few words in Quechua or Aimará and the Indians would hand over the bills that he so dexterously placed between his fingers. It was a scene that was equally laughable and disgusting in its surrealism. Ernesto went to ask the Indians about what was going on. When he came back he told me, "The priest sells them lots in heaven and, depending on how much they spend, some lots are better than others." It was unbelievable, there was even some haggling going on in which they argued the price and the Indian would threaten to walk away, the priest calling him back until they reached an agreement. The guy was taking advantage of the ignorance of the Indians who had mostly come because of their numerous problems—illnesses, family drama, lack of work, etc. Ernesto, who was totally anti-clerical just like me, had his beliefs once again confirmed by the sight of this well-fed priest trading celestial promises for cash from those poor Indians. He surely must have brought in good money every day. Of course, all in the name of greater glory and honor to God ...

The following day we had to leave for Perú and were planning on making the trip by donkey in the morning, but we heard there was a truck that was going that way in the afternoon and decided to wait for it. However, thanks to the number of suitcases we had and how long it took us to gather everything up, we got there too late and the truck had already left, so we had no choice but to make the trip on foot. We hired two Indians to help us with the luggage—poor guys, our bags were bigger than they were, mainly Ernesto's, as he describes with humor:

Between laughing and swearing, we finally reached the hotel. One of the Indians, whom we had named Tupac Amaru, was a sad sight—every time he sat down to rest, we had to help him get back on his feet because he just couldn't on his own. We slept like logs [that night].[27]

On top of everything else, the Indians barely spoke Spanish. We felt really sorry for them, so we helped them to carry the bags and shared our food with them— a delicious meal that our benefactress at the hotel had prepared as a parting gift. It was a comical scene because we were all stumbling along and at one point Ernesto had a laughing fit that spread quickly to all of us. Even the Indians, usually very serious and inexpressive, ended up rolling on the ground laughing. Ernesto had the most contagious laugh I've ever heard in my life.

That night we slept in the border town of Guaqui where we had to have our passports stamped. Since the border guard in charge of that task was famous for his absence, we had a boring wait until the following day. The next morning they signed our passports and we hitched a comfortable ride on a truck that would take us to the Yunguyo area where we crossed over into Perú.

On August 17, 1953 we finally left Bolivia—Ernesto wouldn't return there until years later as Che (disguised as Ramón), where he would be assassinated on October 9, 1967 at age 39. But that was a lifetime away. That first stay in Bolivia, which went from the originally planned one week to more than a month, had been intense, enjoyable and friendly and had taught us much about a poor, indigenous America with an aptitude for revolution. Perú would not receive us in the same way.

---

27 Ib., p. 17.

CHAPTER 4

Perú

The most important thing is that we are here beholding a pure expression of the most powerful indigenous civilization in America, untainted by contact with the conquering armies and rich with immense, evocative treasures held within its dead walls and the stunning landscape that surrounds it—the perfect setting to enrapture the dreamer who wanders among its ruins or the Yankee tourist who, full of practicality, boxes up the evidence of the fallen tribe he finds inside these once living walls, unaware of the moral distance that separates him from them. These are subtleties that only the semi-indigenous spirit of the Latin American can appreciate.

—ERNESTO GUEVARA

Perú was a country with a dilemma much like that of Bolivia. Basically, it had the same unresolved indigenous problem, i.e., the majority of its population was terribly poor, with no education, no healthcare and many other needs. However, while the revolution in Bolivia was taking a step toward solving these problems, Perú lived under a fierce dictatorship led by General Odría, in which social disparity was intensified and the potential for "ideological contamination" from its neighboring country feared above all.

We got a firsthand taste of this right away.

At the last border control in the city of Puno, they went through our luggage and did us the favor of "lightening" the load that had given us so much difficulty on the hike from Bahía de Copacabana. They confiscated two books that Ernesto was carrying—one he had brought from Buenos Aires, *El hombre en la Unión Soviética*, as well as a publication from the Ministry of Peasant Affairs given to us as a gift by Ñuflo Chávez. "It was classified as red, red, red with exclamation points and reproach. After a spirited chat with the chief of police, I agreed to pick up the publication in Lima,"[1] Ernesto notes in his journal. There was no convincing them—no matter how much we protested and argued, they still took the books from us. When we were considered "clean" of all political contamination, they let us officially enter Perú and stamped our passports. It was August 18, 1953.

---

1 E. Guevara, *Otra vez*, p. 17.

We slept that night in a pensión in Puno where we planned our next moves. Ernesto took the command, since he had already been in Perú and his experience gave him the authority to become the indisputable leader of our expedition there. He considered the area between Puno and Cuzco to hold nothing of particular interest for us to see and, therefore, that it was better to travel that stretch by train. We would save time and, if we traveled second-class, money as well.

The following morning we hauled our luggage once again and headed for the station to buy our second-class tickets. There was a strange calm about the nearly deserted station that was more disturbing than peaceful. We went up to the window and asked to buy our tickets. The ticket salesman looked us up and down and said, "No, no—I can't sell you second-class tickets." We asked why, but he couldn't explain what we had already figured out: The second-class cars were the realm of ill-treatment of Indians. What was slowly changing in Bolivia was still the norm in Perú. We saw with our own eyes how the guards—often inebriated—pushed the Indians, kicking them and spitting on them, into the single-doored wagon used for transporting livestock. This was where the elderly, the young, women and children piled on top of each other and animals to travel in an unbearable stench of human and animal excrement. The guards, depending on their whims or their mood, decided whether or not to open the door for the Indians who wanted to get off at each station. They would often leave them closed up, ignoring the passengers' pleas and the train would pull out again only for them to get off kilometers later and quietly begin the walk to their homes or places of work.

We were aware of all this and it was infuriating that the guard should refuse to sell us the tickets just because we were white. We got into an argument, demanding an explanation and he gave evasive answers like, "You can't travel there with all those people, the smell, the crowding ..." After much discussion, Ernesto got angry and said, "Just who the hell do you think you are? You're going to sell me those tickets and that's final. *We* decide how we want to travel." He reminded me of his father that day in the Rayo de Sol when he became so furious with the waiter who refused to heat up Patatín's baby bottle.

"Fine," agreed the ticket seller, "I'll sell them to you at your own risk. The train arrives in four hours—that is, if it arrives on time."

Tickets in hand, we went to have a look around the station and shed our bad mood. Ernesto sat down on the floor and leaned back on the wall to write in his journal. I kept walking along the platform until two guys dressed in suits and ties suddenly confronted me.

"You two have second-class tickets, right?"

"Oh, no—not again! Give me a break with the second-class thing, do you mind! We already got into it once over that, so just leave us the hell alone, damn it! We're traveling in second and that's final," I said; I was fed up with arguing over the bloody tickets.

"Hey, watch your language, buddy! We're Peruvian detectives," they both reacted taking out their credentials.

"Oh ... well, in that case ...," I swallowed and gestured desperately to Ernesto for him to come over. "Look, all our papers are in order, our passports, visas, entry into the country ..."

"No need to go into all that, boys. This isn't about papers; we want to propose a deal."

"A deal? Interesting. What kind of deal?" asked Ernesto, recovering his nerve and becoming businessman-like.

"It's like this: We were supposed to take two convicts

from Puno to Cuzco in the first-class wagon, but unfortunately, they escaped. Since there are two free seats now, we could sell those second-class tickets you've got there, you keep the money from one, we keep what we get for the other and everybody's happy. You travel in first-class and we each earn a little something.

"Okay, why not?" we both responded at the same time, after briefly looking at each other to make sure. It was a good deal—we would travel in first-class for the price of just one second-class ticket.

"Don't start jumping up and down—there's one 'but'," said the two cops. "Since you have to pass for prisoners in front of the guards, you'll have to wear handcuffs …"

"Um … okay," we answered after another quick glance at each other.

So they cuffed us and we somehow managed to lug all our suitcases and board the train, half embarrassed and half laughing. The two policemen sat side-by-side in a double seat with us across from them in our handcuffs. The train pulled away and we became the center of attention. It wasn't a first-class car like the ones in Argentina that we remembered from those trips long ago between Alta Gracia and Buenos Aires. Here there was no luxury and the passengers were financially not much better-off than those traveling in second.

"Would you like a pastry, young man?"

"Or perhaps a chicken leg?"

The signs of camaraderie from the simple people sharing the wagon with us—two poor prisoners fallen from grace—were numerous and moving. They paid no attention whatsoever to the policemen. It was the solidarity of common folk with the weak and their distrust of authority. This was the same throughout Latin America, no matter who controlled the government. The indigenous population often didn't know who governed them; they sometimes weren't even sure about their nationality, lacking proper documents and wandering indiscriminately across borders.

During the trip, we got to talking to the detectives—pigs, as Ernesto liked to call cops—two short and stocky mestizos. He told them that he had just become a doctor, that he had traveled in Perú before and that we were studying the fight against leprosy in South America—the same story as always. In a nutshell, they seemed to like us and one said to the other, "These seem like nice young men—I don't think they need to be handcuffed. I've got an idea—let's give them our I.D.'s; since everyone already knows us, they won't ask us to show our tickets and these two, with the way they look, can easily pass for detectives."

The other guy agreed and they removed our cuffs. We thus went from being criminals in transit one minute to Peruvian police officers with badges the next. Not long after, the conductor came through asking for tickets and we, very nonchalantly, took out our badges and he made a gesture as if to say, "Yeah, yeah—I know why you guys are here" and he kept walking. He must have thought that we were undercover cops dressed as civilians or something.

"Using that little trick, we traveled comfortably in first-class, flashing our badges every time the guard passed by. With this, we put Carlitos Figueroa's infamous I.D. to shame,"[2] Ernesto joked in a letter to Celia. He was referring to the notorious Courts I.D. that Figueroa had managed to get and that he used as a safe-conduct pass whenever he got into a brawl or needed something.

Later on, the real detectives went to another car

---

2 W. Gálvez Rodríguez, Op. cit., p. 238.

where there was gambling and drinking going on. Ernesto went with them to check it out, but I chose to stay in my seat and read. He came back a little later, all worked up and said, "Give me twenty sols—come on, take off the chastity belt.

"What do you want money for? This is crazy—you're gonna lose it," I warned him

"I want to have a go; I think I can win. I can take those guys for all they're worth," he told me, full of himself, I suppose due to our success at the poker table in La Paz that had left us with a few extra pesos in our pockets.

I didn't have any choice but to get up, go to the bathroom and take twenty sols from my chastity belt. He went off with the money and came back an hour later.

"So?" I asked, although his face said it all.

"They screwed me—they played dirty and took me for everything I had." Well, live and learn.

We arrived in Cuzco by night and started looking for the *canas*[3] so we could give them their badges back. We returned one, but when we found the other guy, he was so filthy drunk that they were dragging him out—I remember that he was coming out of his shoes. We didn't worry too much about it and went to look for a place to stay. We found one that was dirtier than usual, but cheap. Our financial situation had become notably worse in Perú. We had by then spent nearly half of the Argentine pesos we carried in the famous belt and the exchange rate here was not favorable like it had been in Bolivia; in fact, it was just the opposite. The luxuries of the "good life" ended for us in Perú.

The following morning, we headed for the police station. This had become part of our regular routine as young travelers in authoritarian Latin America: the

---

3 Cops.

The entry visa for Perú that we obtained in Buenos Aires thanks to our contacts, despite the resistance we experienced in the consulate. Perú was under the dictatorship of General Odría then. At the border, they confiscated two books from Ernesto that they declared to be "red".

obligatory visit to register our names and show our passports at the police station in each town. The commissary in Cuzco was an impressive building with a long stairway at the entrance. As we were walking up, a guy appeared, pointing at us and yelling, "Those are the two who robbed the detective's credentials!"

"Hey, we didn't rob anything!" replied Ernesto, shocked.

"Oh, yeah—you crooks!" they yelled as they grabbed us by the arms.

"Where's the badge?" they demanded roughly or, as

Ernesto put it, "in their characteristically professional tone."[4]

"It's in the hotel—this was all a misunderstanding," I interrupted, trying to calm everyone down.

"Fine, you go and get it, but your friend stays here as collateral," the policeman who was holding Ernesto tightest said threateningly.

So I ran as fast as I could across the city all the way back to the hotel to get the badge and return it to the commissary. When I finally got back, the actual owner of the badge was now present. He dutifully came over to us and said, "Hi, boys—how are you? Please forgive this misunderstanding ... you understand my position ..." And we understood that we had to keep our mouths shut. Clearly, his colleagues couldn't find out that he had lent his badge to two travelers and, furthermore, had lost it due to drunkenness.

"Have you boys ever eaten in a *picantería*?"

"No."

"Well, today I'm taking you out to eat. You'll love it."

That night we met in the picantería, a typical Peruvian restaurant where all sorts of spicy foods are served. The locals would challenge each other to see who could withstand the spiciest dish. It was a sign of masculinity. So the guy said to us, "The first thing I'll treat you to is a nice soup." When they brought it, it was sheer fire. And on top of that, the policeman added even more hot sauce—it was smoking! This was our first time in one of these establishments and, despite our hunger, we could hardly eat a thing, choking on just about everything. Our companion told us that in the days before refrigerators when food went bad quickly, these spices were used to numb the mouth so people wouldn't notice

---

4 E. Guevara, *Otra vez*, p. 18.

the foul taste or smell. As we put all our effort into eating, Ernesto nudged me and gestured toward the open door to the kitchen. There, right in front of everyone, the waiters dumped what was left in peoples' soup bowls back into the pot to then be re-served to the new arrivals. Ernesto, very scientifically and with the authority of his medical diploma, said in a low voice, "Don't worry—go ahead and eat it. All those spices kill any microbes in there—it's like sterilizing the food."

Ernesto was my official guide in Cuzco, having already been there on his first trip with Granado and having read so much on the city. Cuzco had been the capital of the Incan Empire and was founded in the 13th century by the Incan Manco Capac. Its splendor and fame were the origin of the El Dorado legend that brought the avaricious Spanish conquistadors. In 1533, Francisco Pizarro established Spanish dominion over the city. It was the capital of the South American colonies for a century, later replaced by Lima. Cuzco actually remains the capital of Andean Perú, which has become more and more indigenous. In its enclave in the Andean range, the city has a fascinating, eclectic architecture thanks to its history of grandeur, defeat and domination. The churches, whose baroque colonial style the Spaniards imported from Europe, were built on foundations made of Incan ruins. Ernesto enjoyed telling how, whenever one of the earthquakes common to that area occurred, any damage to buildings always happened to the Spanish part, while the Incan remains were always left intact.

For two days, we visited countless churches, each one containing some artistic treasure that the Indians had made at the service of the Spaniards. I remember an altar completely worked in silver or a pulpit carved from the trunk of a tree. "I once again arrange in my head a little collection of altars, enormous paintings and pulpits,"[5] describes Ernesto. He especially liked the pulpit of the church of San Francisco for "its simplicity and serenity", also mentioned in his journal. He was quite happy when, at one of the museums we visited, a museum employee confirmed the authenticity of the statuette he had found on the Isla del Sol and that it was alloyed in the typical Incan technique. He christened it Martha (for Martha Pinilla, his Bolivian girlfriend) and she became a permanent member of our gang. Even though Ernesto had already been there, he showed as much enthusiasm as if it were his first time in Cuzco. In a letter to his friend Tita, he recommended that she visit the city:"I can't urge you enough to visit here as soon as you can and mainly, Machu Picchu. I promise you won't regret it."[6]

We were anxious to get to Machu Picchu, having had our fill of so many churches, but the currency exchange had us trapped. Argentine pesos were not as welcome here as in Bolivia, and we didn't have anything else to offer in exchange for the Peruvian sols that we so needed. Then we met an Argentine woman who promised to get us the exchange. Just as had happened throughout the trip so far, we always ran into Argentine characters in the most unusual places and situations. This woman sold Incan antiques to North American tourists, the ones you could see coming from a mile away in their sloppy clothes, their bermudas, their sandals and cameras around their necks. She supposedly brought the "antiques" personally from expeditions into the old Incan towns. She charged them an arm and a leg, but the

---

5 Ib., p. 18.
6 A. Cupull and F. González, Op. cit., p. 45.

tourists went off happy as clams with their "authentic" relics. As soon as they were back on their tour bus, the woman would re-stock the window with exactly the same false "antiques"—typical criolla[7] shrewdness in the middle of the Andes. We became friends and she took care of us, helped us to plan our trip to Machu Picchu and even gave us two backpacks full of provisions and camping supplies that had belonged to WWII soldiers. The friendship, however, didn't amount to much when it came to getting our money exchanged. She murdered us, giving us 600 sols for our thousand pesos. "Business is business" seemed to be our new friend's motto. "It is true that our hunger is momentarily taken care of,"[8] Ernesto reflected pragmatically.

With the Peruvian sols, we bought two tickets—second-class, of course—from Cuzco to Machu Picchu. There, surrounded by a beautiful landscape as we followed the Urubamba River, we were able to confirm the oft-mentioned inconveniences of the second-class wagon. But we didn't care a bit—we enjoyed the trip anyway aboard that "asthmatic, almost-toy train."[9]

"As pretty as the hills of Córdoba," I declared, just as I did every time I saw a beautiful landscape. And Ernesto laughed at me, saying that I bragged just like a porteño, although I knew he also felt very Cordoban and loved Córdoba. The train left us at the station at the base of the peak atop which Machu Picchu rose. The ascent to the ruins, the famous Camino del Inca, could be done on foot or by bus. The first-class passengers got on the

---

7 Creole (American-born of European descent).
8 E. Guevara, *Otra vez*, p. 18.
9 Ernesto Guevara de la Serna, "Machu Picchu, enigma de piedra en América" in *Otra vez*, p. 137.

shuttles. Ernesto and I decided to go on foot, our youth-fulness allowing us to take on anything. Luckily, we didn't have much to carry, since we had left all our heavy bags with our Argentine friend back in Cuzco. We hiked for several hours along the 8 km of mountainous jungle landscape. Fortunately, Ernesto's asthma didn't bother him despite the steep path. He was in an excellent mood, happy to return to see the ruins that had so impressed him on his first trip. Ernesto was a fantastic travel companion; he was always in a good mood, took everything on with enthusiasm, he was a good conver-sationalist and liked to share what he knew as well as what he had. And clearly, he knew a lot more than I did; whenever he got the chance, he'd stop at a library and read about the places we were going to visit while I wan-dered about always on the look-out for female company. His position as expedition leader was well-deserved, both for his temperament and his knowledge. And he was just basically a good person—his personality reminded me a lot of Celia. He wasn't overly affectionate, but he displayed gestures and attitudes that conveyed affection and made you love him. He also had a positive attitude toward life that bred respect and admiration.

The ruins once again dazzled Ernesto and left their impression upon me as well. "Machu Picchu doesn't let you down. I don't know how many more chances I'll get to admire it, but those grey clouds, those purple and multi-colored summits that highlight the light-grey of the ruins make for one of the most marvelous sights imaginable,"[10] Ernesto wrote that night in his journal. It's an ancient Incan city build on a steep mountain rising out of the Yucay valley. Ernesto showed me around the impressive ruins, 150 buildings that look like giant

---

[10] E. Guevara, *Otra vez*, p. 18.

abstract sculptures all connected by stairways and passageways. It was impossible to visit the sight and not feel a profound sense of admiration for the people who had erected such a city in the middle of a mountain range. The fact that it had remained standing and not been flattened by Spanish churches and monuments must have been due to the difficult access, leaving it to be forgotten, and the vegetation which did its job to hide it for many years. Until 1912, when it was discovered by a North American explorer, Hiram Bingham, the city was completely overgrown with weeds and not even visible from planes flying over. Once they got all the overgrowth off, they discovered an unbelievably intact city. Of course, imperialism went into action and proceeded to take all the Incan artifacts discovered to the United States. Ernesto describes this reality in an article published in the Panamanian magazine *Siete* in December of that same year:

> The ruins were left free of weeds, perfectly studied and described and ... totally stripped of any objects the researchers got their hands on. They triumphantly took more than 200 boxes full of priceless archeological treasures that were also—why not say so— worth a lot of money ... Where can the treasures of this indigenous city now be admired or studied? The answer is obvious: in U.S. museums.[11]

The magnificence of Machu Picchu incited Ernesto's pan-American and pro-indigenous sentiment and his visceral rejection of all types of imperialism, whether it be the Spanish conquistador with his sword and cross or U.S. dominance with its economic and military might.

---

11 E. Guevara, "Machu Picchu..." in *Otra vez*, p. 136.

He poured all of the feelings awoken in him during that visit onto the pages of the article in *Siete;* just like nearly everything else that happened on that trip, the significance of that visit went way beyond the merely tourist.

> The most important thing is that we are here beholding a pure expression of the most powerful indigenous civilization in America, untainted by contact with the conquering armies and rich with immense, evocative treasures held within its dead walls and the stunning landscape that surrounds it— the perfect setting to enrapture the dreamer who wanders among its ruins or the Yankee tourist who, full of practicality, boxes up the evidence of the fallen tribe he finds inside these once living walls, unaware of the moral distance that separates him from them. These are subtleties that only the semi-indigenous spirit of the Latin American can appreciate.[12]

Ernesto already identified himself fully as Latin American[13] and felt a kinship with the indigenous people who, until just recently, had been so alien to us both. He concluded the article with a poetic description of what Machu Picchu meant for him:

> ... for the fighter who goes after what today is called chimera, the one with his arm extended toward the future and his voice of stone whose cry reaches across continents: "Citizens of Indo-America, reconquer your past."[14]

---

12 Ib., p. 138.
13 Translator's note: The implication here is "not merely Argentine."
14 E. Guevara, "Machu Picchu..." in *Otra vez*, p. 139.

Another photo that shows Ernesto's skill as a photographer. Here I am in Machu Picchu wearing my famous López Taibo boots. Ernesto wrote in his journal: "Machu Picchu doesn't let you down. I don't know how many more chances I'll get to admire it, but those grey clouds, those purple and multi-colored summits that highlight the light-grey of the ruins make for one of the most marvelous sights imaginable."

In our enthusiasm, we had wanted to scale Huayna Picchu ('new peak'), which faces Machu Picchu ('old peak') and is much steeper. The summit held, in addition to smaller Incan ruins, a bottle containing notes written by Ernesto and Alberto that they had buried one year before and sworn to unearth if either should ever return there. The weather, however, wasn't good and we decided in the end not to risk the 400-meter climb.

Our other task in Machu Picchu was a bit more prosaic, but nonetheless necessary. We intended to sleep for free, a difficult enterprise considering that the only accommodation near the ruins was a luxury hotel for international tourism. Movie stars the likes of Joan Fontaine stayed there. Everything we had left in our chastity belt didn't amount to enough to pay for one night in a room there. However, Ernesto and Alberto had met the hotel manager on the previous trip and had made a good impression thanks to an on-the-spot soccer match amid the ruins, in which Ernesto had played a stand-out game as goalie.

"The manager's name is Soto," Ernesto explained, "and he's a Peruvian admirer of Argentines because he loves tango and soccer. He sings like crap, likewise for his soccer playing, but all you have to do is tell him how good he is at both and we're home-free. It's a well-intentioned lie," he told me, excusing himself for this one exception to his usual policy of absolute honesty that had brought us so many problems. Machu Picchu was worth the exception.

In the 1950s, being Argentine was like a letter of introduction to the rest of Latin America. We inspired affection as well as a bit of envy. Argentine soccer and the tango were in their heyday, along with cinema and Peronism—all were a source of conversation and allowed you to come across as someone interesting. It was hard for me to believe, because my background had taught me that Argentines were well-known for things like our Nobel prize-winners, Carlos Saavedra Lamas and Bernardo Houssay. However, along the way I realized that we were more known for Gardel, Sandrini, Enrique Serrano, the Legrand twins, Hugo del Carril, our soccer stars and for Perón. For Ernesto and I, raised as anti-Peronists, it was odd how much admiration Perón inspired outside of Argentina. He was seen as a champion of anti-imperialism who had gotten the better of the son-of-a-bitch Braden, the famous U.S. ambassador who had supported Perón's opposition and been part of extremely imperialist U.S. companies like United Fruit. Gringo-resentment in the rest of Latin America was much more accentuated than in Argentina. "Perón really has balls, confronting the U.S. like that!" they would say.

Fortunately for us, this guy Soto remembered Ernesto well and welcomed us with open arms. "Here I am again," Ernesto said, "on another trip, this time with my friend Carlos Ferrer. As usual, we're flat broke ..."

Soto understood right away and didn't make us beg, "Don't worry, boys—for a couple of sols I'll put you up in one of the hotel maid's quarters." So that's how we ended up sleeping "in semi-luxury"[15], as Ernesto put it. That maid's room was better than any place we had stayed the whole trip; it had two beds with mattresses, clean sheets and a bathroom nearby—total luxury. That night, our friend Soto butchered a few tangos with me accompanying him on several wrong notes. Ernesto, who, as I already mentioned, had a cigar stuck in each ear, listened to us completely immune to the musical travesty we were perpetrating. (I got a good laugh years later when I learned that the revolutionary guerrillas who were with him in the jungle would cover their ears whenever he sang, saying, "The commander's at it again, assassinating another tango.") Ernesto stayed to chat with the manager, who knew a lot about Inca civilization.

The following day, true to our word, we gave Soto the pleasure of a little pick-up game in the ruins at the Plaza de Armas. The Indians brought a ball and Ernesto played goalkeeper. Ever since Alta Gracia, he had always played goalie, at first because his asthma kept

---

15 Letter from Ernesto to his mother, August 22, 1953. W. Gálvez Rodríguez, Op. cit., p. 238.

him from running, but later because he had become outstanding at the position. He had no fear—he was a daring player capable of diving at the feet of whoever was carrying the ball, even it they were twice his weight.

"Don't run too much—the altitude will kill you," he warned me. I told him casually and with all the self-importance of my 24 years not to worry, that I knew what I had to do. I began playing with everything I had and, just like he said, after ten minutes I was done for. Ernesto, on the other hand, played fantastically as goalie and upheld the good name of Argentines as great soccer players, even though he let Soto score one or two goals. When it was over, he said, "See, man—I told you it was better to play goalie instead of running like an idiot."

We sadly bid farewell to Machu Picchu and to Soto and his hotel. When we went to sign the guest book, we found a comment written by a tourist in English that seemed equally ironic and profound: "I am lucky to find a place without Coca-Cola propaganda." In December, Ernesto used that line to close his article on Machu Picchu for *Siete* and sarcastically stated that it had been written by an "English subject … with all the bitterness of his imperial longing."[16]

After an experience as intense as the one in Machu Picchu, Cuzco didn't seem all that attractive. At least not for me—the filth became a matter of obsession for me. We went back to the same pensión that now seemed even more wretched than before. The beds we slept on had mattresses that hadn't been shaken for decades that were sunken in the middle by the countless bodies that had slept there. The sheet seemed more like a blanket because of the accumulated grime on it. And under the bed, the urinal sported souvenirs left by other travelers.

---

16 E. Guevara, "Machu Picchu…" in *Otra vez*, p. 139.

"I'm not even taking my boots off," I told Ernesto before going to bed and I really did lay down fully dressed, even my hat. He did the same, but as a joke.

"Too bad we didn't bring the Vendaval!" he joked, laughing as he watched me squirm because of the bugs and lice swarming all over us. Vendaval was that insecticide that he and Carlos Figueroa had manufactured, nearly poisoning the entire family. On top of all that, our stay in Cuzco was prolonged because we couldn't find a trucker willing to give us a ride to Lima. We ended up spending eight days there, while our sols quickly ran out. What was worse, we had to resort to our Argentine "friend" to exchange our money. So we decided to ration our expenses to an extreme. One day, I couldn't take it anymore and I told Ernesto I wanted a bath even though I'd have to go pay at one of the public bathhouses, I was so sweaty and smelly.

"Oh, no! That's superfluous!" he exclaimed, annoyed. "You have your allowance for the day, so choose: either you eat or you bathe." I was so obstinate about the bath that I chose to be clean rather than to eat that day. Of course, once I had bathed, my good humor returned ... along with my hunger. Ernesto had gone to eat at an inn and his table was covered with little plates of different foods they typically serve in Perú. As he nibbled on one dish after another with pleasure, I sat down in front of him and looked longingly at the food. But I wasn't about to ask him for any and he continued eating as if he didn't notice. He finally nodded towards the food and said, "Go ahead, have some, you big jerk. Now you see that eating is more important than being all clean?" And then he shared everything with me. That was Ernesto, generous beyond comparison. As I ate, I remembered the days when he treated our whole gang to sandwiches in Alta Gracia, spending what little he had.

"Little by little our hopes are whittled away as the days pass and our pesos or sols dwindle,"[17] he wrote of our days of waiting in Cuzco. One day we were about to get a ride in a truck headed for Lima with our bags loaded and ready to go, but then the driver made us get out because we weren't willing to pay the amount he asked. We thought it was outrageous—much more expensive than the bus.

To kill the boredom, we went to see a psychic our Argentinean friend had told us about. The encounter was hilarious. In Ernesto's words:

> The guy gave us some weird reports on some lights he saw coming from us—the green light of affection and selfishness in Calica, and the dark green of adaptability in me. Then he asked me if I had anything in my stomach because he saw that my radiations were a bit low, which got me to thinking, "Yeah, because my stomach's complaining about all those Peruvian stews and canned food."[18]

We laughed about the psychic, but the truth was he had a point—my spirit of sacrifice had begun to reach its limit in Cuzco, while Ernesto seemed to adapt to anything without complaint. Our differences of personality were highlighted those days and we decided to get bus tickets and head for Lima once and for all to get back our enthusiasm for traveling. We both wrote home.

"Cuzco is interesting, but it's the dirtiest city you could imagine. So much so, that you just have to bathe. During the eight days we spent here, el Chancho took one bath and that was by mutual agreement, just for

---

17 E. Guevara, *Otra vez*, p. 19.
18 Ib., p. 19.

health reasons," I joked in a letter to my mother.

Ernesto, as for his part, wrote to Celia:

Alberto would throw himself on the ground to marry Incan princesses and reclaim empires. Calica gripes about the filth and every time he steps on one of the numerous turds strewn about the streets, instead of looking toward the sky and seeing a cathedral cut out of the clouds, he looks at a his dirty shoes. He doesn't smell that impalpable substance evoked by Cuzco, but rather the smell of stew and manure. It's really a matter of temperaments. We've decided to quickly get out of here considering how little he likes the city.

In the same letter he describes what he thought would be his steps in the near future:

Of my future, I won't say anything because I don't know, not even how things will go in Venezuela ... Further along, I will say that I'm still counting on earning US$10,000 for another possible Latin American trip with Alberto, this time from north to south, maybe by helicopter. Then on to Europe; beyond that it's all blank.[19]

The trip by bus to Lima lasted approximately three days. In reality, the "bus" was an old, broken-down wreck of a contraption with wooden seats and—the ultimate in comfort—a stretch of canvas that served as both seating and roof. We traveled among the chickens and calves, stopping often for people to get on and off. Even Ernesto, with his unforgettable endurance, commented

---

19 W. Gálvez Rodríguez, Op. cit., p. 239.

on the precariousness of our transport. "The trip was eternal. The chickens had shit the seat directly above us, creating an unbearable stench so thick you could slice it with a knife."[20] To get a breath of air and admire the landscape, we'd venture up onto the canvas roof every so often. The scenery was beautiful as we traveled along the Apurimac River and over countless mountains and valleys. The roads were precarious and dangerous, carved out of the rock slopes leaving just enough space for vehicles to pass. If two trucks met coming from opposite directions, one would have to back up and let the other through first. Then there was the threat of landslides, which were frequent. Several times we were forced to stop because a landslide had blocked the road; we'd wait for them to send word for a tractor to come and clear off the road. After a few hours, the tractor would show up and begin its very risky job of moving the rocks out of the road, working in muddy terrain caused by the natural springs that were usually the source of the landslide. And of course, this involved the risk of another landslide occurring on top of the tractor. Ernesto and I admired the skill and calmness of the Indians and mestizos who handled this difficult job.

The bus and truck drivers were also excellent at their jobs. They drove on that extremely dangerous terrain in old vehicles with unsafe brakes, worn-out tires and no shocks. Perhaps because of the experience of his first trip or perhaps it was simply due to his courage, Ernesto was completely confident. I, on the other hand, was constantly watching the brakes, the curves, the crater-like potholes. At one point, we were riding on the roof and talking when the bus entered an extremely narrow road with tight curves. On a turn, one of the wheels came

---

20 E. Guevara, *Otra vez*, p. 19.

nearly off the ground. I was petrified and began to yell, "We're going over the edge!"

"Relax, no we won't. Don't worry," Ernesto tried to calm me down. I insisted that we were going over and in my desperation, I jumped off the top of the bus and landed in the mud. Ernesto, who remained atop the fishtailing bus with one of its wheels on the edge of the cliff, yelled down at me laughing, "You chicken shit from Córdoba!"

However, even he couldn't take it when the driver stopped and asked, "Anybody know how to drive?" No one said anything, including us; one thing was driving a car—a broken-down truck in the middle of the mountains was another. He drove a bit further and then asked again, "Nobody here knows how to drive? I'm getting really sleepy and if no one will drive, we won't be able to go on." Faced with the prospect of taking on those curves with a half-asleep driver, one of the passengers volunteered to take the wheel. The driver stretched out on one of the seats to sleep until we reached the next town and, fully recovered, re-took the wheel. That was what our "bus" to Lima was like.

The "catering" on our bus was also a matter of improvisation. We offered to help load bags or animals onto the bus in exchange for a tamal or a glass of juice. And at the stops, there was always someone there offering a plate of rice with hot sauce; if you were patient enough to wait your turn to use the only spoon and plate, you could enjoy a good meal for nearly nothing. And to drink, the best thing was the pisco, because the water wasn't clean and could make you sick. Pisco also helped to fight off the bitter cold up in the mountains. As the bus went up and down mountains, the climate changed radically. In the morning you could be freezing with all your warm clothes on, and then by the afternoon you'd have to go stripping off layers because of the heat. I put on and took off the coat that, along with my boots, was my other source of pride on that trip.

"As soon as it gets really hot, I'm going to sell it," I would say to Ernesto.

"Well, you'll have to sell it for a couple of pesos then, because nobody needs a coat where it's hot."

On one of the stops in the heat of the day, we decided to take a swim in a pretty backwater of the river. Of course we had no swimming trunks, so we had to skinny dip. The water (spring thaw) was as cold as an iceberg. Suddenly, we realized that all the other passengers, including the women, were watching us. I managed to cover my privates, but Ernesto, ready for a little scandal, began jumping around like a monkey in his birthday suit. It was a fun-filled moment, although the cold water wasn't good for Ernesto's asthma and he had to resort to his inhaler. Fortunately, it didn't go any further than that. Attacks like the one he had in La Quiaca didn't reoccur throughout the rest of our trip.

When we stopped for the night, we would sleep under the bus or in any little shack near the road where they'd give us a corner. In each place, we found the same quiet poverty. We wanted to know everything about how the Indians lived, but it was difficult to break the barrier with them—they were extremely reserved and many didn't even speak Spanish. For this reason, I was surprised when on one part of the journey while I was dozing, I was woken by the laughter of Ernesto and an Indian with whom he was having a lively conversation in another seat. As I've mentioned, Ernesto had a contagious laugh and he was very ingenious, but it was rare to see an Indian laugh. The Indian was telling him in his broken Spanish that he had to make a four-day journey to visit a relative and his only provisions were a little bag of cooked chickpeas that he ate a little at a time. He shared a handful with Ernesto, who in gratitude took out a can of sardines to share from the provisions in the backpacks given to us by our "antique-dealer" friend in Cuzco. When he opened the can, a stream shot out all the way to the ceiling of the bus. Ernesto went on preparing his crackers and sardines as if nothing had happened.

"You're not planning on eating that? Didn't you see what just shot out of that can? They're bad—that could kill a horse!"

"Of course I'm going to eat it—they're fine," he argued as he continued spreading the crackers for his little picnic right there in the bus.

"But listen to me, you shithead—your mother left me in charge of looking out for you. And you're gonna eat that can from 1940, you're gonna get food poisoning here in the middle of the jungle and we won't even be able to find a medicine man to cure you. You'll die, man, and then what am I supposed to do with your dead body?"

"No, you'll see that nothing at all's going to happen to me. Sure you don't want some?" And he ate those sardines just like that and so did the Indian. For dessert, they had some chocolate that had gone all chalky that he found in the bottom of the backpack. At least they were from the Second and not the First World War, I thought. I couldn't bring myself to eat and was left with a hole in my stomach while they had a happy little feast. The minutes went by with me glancing over at them to see if the first signs of food poisoning appeared, but they continued talking earnestly. Finally, I fell asleep regretting that I hadn't taken at least a bite. (I remembered this anecdote years later when I read how his comrades in the Sierra Maestra had started the rumor that Che was immortal because he seemed to defy all the dangers around him.)

Something that really stood out throughout that trip was the armed militia. Perú lived under a dictatorship and was clearly militarized. Everything was controlled—we, as foreigners, had to show our passports in every little town we went through. The population, largely indigenous, lived a life of submission with no expectations for change. Just as we were able to see the mistreatment of Indians on the train, that bus trip taught us that the life of an Indian was worth very little in Perú. At one point in the journey, Ernesto and his new friend went up onto the roof; I stayed in the bus. All of a sudden, I heard Ernesto yell to the driver, "Stop, stop! The Indian fell off on the curve!" And the guy kept driving as if nothing had happened. "Hey, stop—a passenger has fallen off!" I intervened.

"No, I don't stop for nobody," the driver answered. Neither Ernesto's nor my indignant protests did any good—he kept on driving until the next stop. While we were there, the Indian showed up on foot, all scratched up. The poor guy's luggage was still on the bus (including his precious chickpeas.) Ernesto was happy to see that he was okay and he cleaned up his wounds as best he could. I was sure that the Indian would cause a scene and let the driver have it, but no: the guy, just as resigned and docile as ever, just got back on as if nothing had happened. That's how they were, living in complete desperation without a shred of hope that a single soul on this earth would ever help them. The only thing they believed in was their religion that mixed the Catholicism brought by the conquistadors with pre-Columbian indigenous creeds. They accepted the Odría dictatorship just like all the other disgraces that befell them.

We also met other adventurers on our trip who were wandering about Latin America just like us. Ernesto was impressed by the story of a Frenchman and took note of it in his journal:

> We met a French explorer on the bus whose boat had sunken on the Apurimac and the current had taken his travel companion, who he at the time claimed was a professor, but turned out to be a student who had run away from home with him and, unfortunately, didn't know how to swim either. This guy's going to be in deep shit.[21]

Finally, after three days and "several flat tires which made the trip even longer, we arrived in Lima and slept like logs in another dive of a hotel."[22] We were quite a wreck when we got to the city. Our outlook improved once there—mine, by momentarily improving our situation thanks to Gogo Nougués, who we had arranged to meet; and Ernesto's, by seeing Dr. Hugo Pesce, a renowned leprosy doctor and acknowledged communist who had given Ernesto help, advice and friendship on his last visit there. We were successful on both counts.

Lima represented a big change in the landscape of our trip. A flat, coastal city, it is full of history, having been the most important capital of South America during Spanish domination. This left not only a significant impact in terms of architecture, but as Ernesto describes after his first visit there with Alberto: "Lima fully represents a Perú that has not emerged from its feudal colonial state; it is still waiting for the blood of a truly emancipating revolution."[23]

When he returned there with me one year later, things

---

21 Ib., p. 19.
22 Ib., p. 19.
23 E. Guevara, *Diarios de motocicleta*, p. 190.

had not changed in the least. Compared to the political effervescence we had witnessed in Bolivia, here we didn't find any opposition to the fierce dictatorship. That is, with the exception of Dr. Pesce, who, despite his political ideas, was respected by the government, both for his professional expertise as well as for his position in the Freemasonry, said to be higher even than General Odría's. Ernesto describes the impression Lima gave him this time around in a letter to his friend Tita: "It seems Yankee domination hasn't even given Perú that false sense of economic well-being apparent, for example, in Venezuela."[24]

Pesce was the first person we went to visit when we arrived. He treated Ernesto with much affection that was also extended to me. He welcomed us into the leprosy section of the Hospital de Guía as well as his home, where we were invited several times for dinner. Ernesto liked talking to him and enjoyed "his conversation, so comprehensive and easy—he speaks with such self-confidence about a variety of topics."[25] Not to mention that his wife, Soraya Sheier, was an excellent cook and his boys, Lucho and Tito, added a note of childish fun to our evenings together.

Those first days in Lima, we had an experience that showed us firsthand, once again, the dictatorship that that country was living under at the time. When we got back to our hotel, we discovered all our belongings upended and two policemen waiting for us, this time not nearly as pleasant and willing to negotiate as those in Puno. They very brusquely asked us for our passports and visas. Ernesto began reciting our trusty alibi for the trip, "I'm an Argentine doctor and my friend, who is an advanced medical student, is here with me studying the fight against leprosy ..."

---

24 A. Cupull and F. González, Op. cit., p. 45.
25 E. Guevara, *Otra vez*, p. 20.

"That makes no difference to us," the cop cut him off. "You'll have to come with us."

"No, you can't take me, I have to talk to the consul first," said Ernesto.

"You're not going anywhere. You're both coming with us."

"But why? What are we being accused of?" I protested.

"You're coming with us and that's final," one of them ordered, making it clear that explanations were a luxury only permitted under democratic governments.

They took us to the police station where we were questioned about everything right down to our shoe size. 'What do you do? Where are you going? Who do you know?' After the interrogation, they locked us up for two hours without explanation. Ernesto and I racked our brains speculating about what might be the motive behind our detention. Could it have anything to do with those books they confiscated from Ernesto at the border in Puno? Could they know about our contacts with the revolutionary government in Bolivia? Did Ernesto's friendship with Pesce put us under suspicion? Finally, the policemen came to let us out of the cells and their tone had changed. After a few apologies, they explained that they were actually looking for an Argentine who had fled with the daughter he had had with a Peruvian woman. The story was not very credible, because if he had fled with a minor, why remain in Perú? He logically would have gotten her out of the country. There was very little reason to believe them and a whole lot more to distrust them. In the middle of a dictatorship, those hours in the commissary could be interpreted as a warning. Just in case, we decided not to go get the books they had confiscated from Ernesto and promised to return to him in Lima.

We went back to the hotel fearing the worst, i.e., that they had made off with all our things, which may have been a mess, but we needed it all. As luck would have it, everything was there. To celebrate, we went to have a bath that we had to pay separately, taking turns waiting outside to guard each other's clothes or otherwise they'd disappear. Once we were looking more presentable, we went to make another house call. Zoraida Boluarte was a social worker in the Hospital de Guía; Ernesto and Alberto had met her on the first trip and she had protected and helped them. Speaking of our visit to her home, she told Cuban journalist Marta Rojas about her happiness at seeing him again:

> When I heard the bell and went to see who was at the door, who should it be? Ernesto with another young man, Carlos Ferrer, with a tremendous beard, which was very uncommon in those days. My whole family was really glad to see him again. We had a long chat in which he told us about his graduation and that he was headed to meet up with Granado. During the conversation, he showed lots of photos from the previous trip, among which there was one that my father and brothers found quite funny, but they wouldn't show me. Given their uncontrollable laughter, I insisted on knowing the cause until they finally told me that when Granado had had a bad case of upset stomach on that trip, Ernesto had taken a picture of him from behind just as he was having one of his many bouts of diarrhea.[26]

Thanks to her, we were able to solve the housing problem that was becoming more of a concern as our capital was slowly eaten up. She told us that the room in the hospital that the travelers had been lent on the

---

26 W. Gálvez Rodríguez, Op. cit., p. 241.

last trip was occupied at the moment and there was no space in her house, but she would find something. "My *ches* can't possibly stay in a crummy hotel," she told us. *Ches* was the nickname the patients at the leper colony had affectionately given Ernesto and Alberto for their warmth and care. Keeping to her word, the following day she found us a room at the house of one of the hospital nurses, the Peirano family, who lived in a large and comfortable house.

"The days have gone by without much chance for anything new," writes Ernesto in his journal, demonstrating that the small diversions and minor events that for me were more than enough, for him were not satisfactory; his spirit was begging for bigger things. "The only thing to speak of is our change of residence, which allows us to live for free. Our new lodgings are terrific. We've already caught a party in which I couldn't drink because of the asthma, but Calica really tied one on."

The other thing he "caught" in rapid conquest, but doesn't mention, was the nurse. And we made friends with the whole family, going out with her, her brothers and cousins, all of whom lived in the same house. One of them was a novice bullfighter—just like in México and Venezuela, bullfights are popular in Perú. One afternoon we went into his room and saw his torero suit all laid out on the bed for the important *corrida* coming up the next day. It was fantastic, full of embroidery and sparkles. The guy was nervous, because he was anxious to become a full-fledged torero, the press having already praised him and talked about his potential and skill. Ernesto got the idea of taking our picture dressed as toreros and asked if he'd mind. We had a good laugh trying on that tight suit and taking snapshots of each other—snapshots that we never developed due to our lack of funds. Ernesto had everyone in stitches as he crossed the room imitating the gestures of bullfighters, and then as a finale, he threw the three-corned hat they use to salute the judges onto the bed. Suddenly, the young bullfighter, who up until that point had watched us with a condescending smile as if we were kids playing dress-up, jumped up, pale with rage, "What have you done!" he screamed, out of his mind. "Now the bull will kill me tomorrow!"

"What did I do?" asked Ernesto, who had no idea what was going on.

"He'll kill me, he'll kill me!" he repeated miserably.

"It's just that for bullfighters, throwing the hat onto a bed is a bad omen," his sister explained.

And if anyone is superstitious in this world, it's toreros. They have all sorts of amulets and rituals to protect them when facing the bull: big medallions, little metals, candles lit for this virgin and that, strict rituals for dressing before the fight. They're extremely complicated fellows. The guy decided that he wasn't going to fight and that was it. We spent hours trying to convince him to fight the next day, hiding our laughter at all his cautionary measures so as not to offend him. His manager begged him to carry through with his commitment, given that he had already been paid in part and had to collect the remainder. Ernesto gave him rational arguments to prove to him that his superstitions were just silly. In the end, either due to the money or common sense, he decided to fight. And it was a complete success. That night we had another party to celebrate his victory, which turned into a real booze bash with everyone getting falling-down drunk. At one point, things got out of hand when one of the other bullfighters tried to steal the host's girlfriend and punches started flying between the two groups.

"We have to get into this—we'll fight for the house," Ernesto told me, ready to take them on. Very sure of ourselves, we pulled out all our boxing skills; however, we didn't count on one detail: Peruvians fight using their fists as well as their heads. Our faces ended up a total wreck, but we finally managed to kick them out of the house. The party went on in insane peace until the wee hours.

Something that put Ernesto into a really bad mood was not receiving letters from his family. Nearly two months had gone by since our departure from Buenos Aires and he was feeling homesick. He reproached his father:

> I expected to find a pile of letters waiting for me here, but to my surprise, there was only yours ... What really bothers me is not receiving any news from home, particularly from Beatriz [his aunt], who I haven't gotten one single letter from and I have no idea where she's headed .... No word whatsoever from Mom, except what I hear from Dolly (her letters *do* arrive). Tell Mom that every time she feels the need for a game of solitaire, for her to write to me before playing; I won't receive any more letters, but at least she won't bother everyone there so much with her solitaire games.... If you have a clear con- science about it, you can write me General Delivery. A big hug for all.[27]

Ernesto was also reunited with the hospital patients who had not forgotten him. For the lepers there, Ernesto was like a god of hope—a young, unbiased doctor, a researcher. "Doctor, let's hope they find something more effective against leprosy," they would say to him full of hope. Ernesto treated them as a doctor, but mostly he

---

27 Ib., p. 243 and 244.

just talked with them and touched them. I believe this was better than any therapy, because they are completely marginalized by society. We went every day to the leper hospital to eat in the university cafeteria which was really cheap, and then we'd spend several hours with the patients talking about soccer, tango and the movies. They were interested in everything. Once, we took them some back-issues of *El Gráfico* sent from Buenos Aires and they couldn't believe it—they were so grateful. In general, they were young people with little means—leprosy was a disease of the poor that set them off on a vicious cycle with no way out: because of their illness, they could not work. I began to lose my fear of the disease, but was still apprehensive and wouldn't shake their hands or hug them the way Ernesto did. The patients there had mild cases of the disease that you could barely notice at first glance; the more advanced cases were deferred to leper colonies far away, like the one at San Pablo that he had visited with Granado.

A few days after our arrival in Lima, we met up with Gogo Nougués as planned. Once again, he treated us incredibly well. Just like in La Paz, our lives began to alternate between visits to the leper hospital and living on a shoestring and our decadent outings with Gogo. Through him, we met the elite members of Peruvian society. Whenever he was invited to a dinner or party, he took us along as his "two traveling nephews." We carefully ate like camels just back from the desert. If anyone noticed, Gogo would just say, "Boys their age, you know ..." As always, I was more enthused with this type of outing than Ernesto, who at that point considered them nearly for "health" reasons, (i.e., they covered our nutritional needs). In a letter I wrote to my mother on September 8th: "Gogo has introduced us to society here, we've eaten twice at the country club—fantastic, cost a fortune, of course we didn't pay a cent—and we've been to the Gran Hotel Bolivar several times."

This Peruvian high society was much more conservative and unyielding than the one in La Paz. Here, there was no interesting night life like the Gallo de Oro, much less political discussions. The upper class completely supported the dictator Odría. I was prepared to break one of his ribs if Ernesto started to argue as he liked to do, because this time it just wasn't possible. It would have been like peeing in bed—there was no room for dissent. It was all clear to Ernesto and he even said to me, "Don't even mention Pesce's name outside of the leper hospital, because he's a communist." In Bolivia we had experienced just the opposite, i.e., the moneyed classes often had to hide their political views because the power lay in the hands of a leftist government.

At one of these get-togethers that Gogo invited us to, we ran into El Gordo Rojo again, who had come from La Paz by plane and planned, as we did, to continue on to Ecuador. He had experienced the same difficulties at the border as we had "but even more so due to the books he was carrying,"[28] Ernesto notes in his journal.

The atmosphere in these circles was plainly neither pleasant nor stimulating for us. To begin with, there were no romances like the one Ernesto had had with the Pinilla girl in La Paz. Our sexual frustrations had to be vented elsewhere. A male nurse at the hospital gave us a hint as to how.

"And how are you fellows doing?" he asked over lunch one day.

"Well... the truth is, things are a little slow," we acknowledged.

---

28 E. Guevara, *Otra vez*, p. 21.

"Here in Lima there are some great *quilombos*[29]. You have three prices: one, two and three sols."

Ernesto and I decided that we had to go "unload", even though we were really low on money. We went to the barrio the nurse had told us about, prepared to close our eyes and go at it with whatever cost one sol. The place was amazing—an entire block full of prostitutes waiting for clients in rooms that gave onto the street with doors split in half like horse stalls. You would go along, making your choice and negotiating the details through the upper part of the door that was open and, once the deal was made, you went in and the door was closed. We started to walk, looking at each other—each one was worse than the one before, but in the end we decided to go ahead with it.

"Anything bigger than a mosquito is game," Ernesto said, winking to encourage me. The one I ended up with was a sort of hippopotamus and, apparently, Ernesto's wasn't any better. We met outside a little later, both pretty depressed with the experience. For a laugh, we began to compete to see which of the two "pros" was the uglier. On top of everything else, two guys started to hassle us because of my beard, which was a phenomenon everywhere we went, since both Indians and mestizos are hairless. "Bah, bah," they yelled at me, imitating a goat and laughing at us because they had seen us go into the one-sol area, famous for its disastrous whores. As worn out as we were, we faced them anyway, ready for a fight, but luckily they chickened out and ran off. That time, we were spared the head-butts.

We went to have a pisco to drown our sorrows and Ernesto, better at seeing the brighter side, advised me, "Don't worry, these things have to happen—it's a health matter." A little high on pisco, we decided to go for a

---

29 Brothels.

162

rematch and try our luck with the three-sol girls. Things went much better that time around and we were able to get our spirits back up. Being young and Argentinean, the *putas* really liked us and did their work with a bit more of a personal touch.

"Come back anytime!" they said as we left.

We began to think of leaving Lima, but once again there was the issue of getting transportation and finding a contact in Ecuador who could lend us a hand and compensate for our nearly non-existent funds. I felt happier in Lima than Ernesto. Our different tastes and personalities were again brought to light. While I wrote to my mother how much "I liked the city, so modern, clean and with all the amenities of a great city", Ernesto wrote in his journal, "The listless days go by as our own inertia keeps us in this city longer than desired."[30] He wasn't even entertained by the strolls and visits to churches and museums accompanied by Zoraida and her family. In his journal he notes stonily:

> Its churches, full of magnificence inside, don't compare to—in my opinion—the august sobriety of the Cuzco temples on the outside. The cathedral contains several scenes of the Passion of Christ done by a painter who would appear to be of the Dutch school, extremely valuable; but I don't like the nave or the exterior style which seems a bit amorphous, as if it were built in a period of transition when Spain's enthusiasm for war began to wane only to be replaced by a love of luxury and comfort. San Pedro has several very valuable paintings, but I don't like the interior there either.[31]

---

30 E. Guevara, *Otra vez*, p. 20.
31 Ib., p. 20 and 21.

In contrast to my own, his spirit was much more at home in an indigenous city like Cuzco than in a great metropolis like Lima.

We were more than two months into the trip and the question of purpose came up more and more often. Ernesto felt that he was spinning in a vacuum with no clear direction. Officially, our destination was Venezuela and reuniting with Granado—a turning point for us to continue traveling the world; he expressed it this way in all the letters to family and friends. Nevertheless, he clearly was no longer comfortable with this objective. One source of concern was his not contributing financially to the family. To his father he writes:

> It's good to know that money's not so tight that you need any urgent help from me. It's good for all of you and for me; this way I can keep going slowly toward the north and everything will be alright, but don't hesitate to let me know if things start to get rough to hurry me along.[32]

"We're here waiting with hardly anything left to see in Lima … Maybe tomorrow (Monday), we'll finally decide about tickets and set a definite departure date,"[33] he writes impatiently. Meanwhile, Zoraida continued to shower us with attention, inviting us to dinner, making us her famous homemade jam that Ernesto had so enjoyed on his previous trip and showing us around with her brothers. Zoraida tells another anecdote related to my beard (which Ernesto envied, since he was nearly hairless despite the fact that he has gone down in history as a member of the *barbudos*[34]

---

32 W. Gálvez Rodríguez, Op. cit., p. 243.
33 E. Guevara, *Otra vez*, p. 20.
34 Bearded ones; used to refer to Cuban revolutionaries.

and that the most famous image, the one taken by Korda, is of Che with a beard): "Of all the different walks we took, one day we went to the port and Calica's beard caused such a sensation that all the little kids began to follow us. It seems they thought we were part of a circus; in the end, we had to hurry out of there."[35]

A letter from Celia dated September 17th put an end to our indecisiveness about leaving. In it she announced to Ernesto that she had supposedly arranged for us to meet the president of Ecuador, Velasco Ibarra. The President's wife was Argentine and that was the source of the Guevara connection. The prospect was a nice one, and also a relief to finally get out of the dictatorial climate of Perú and get to a democratic country. I wrote to my mother again telling her the good news and assuring her candidly that "new horizons awaited us in terms of room and board in Ecuador." I had no idea what really awaited us. Hard times yet to come.

We only had to organize our departure and say goodbye to all the people who had lent us their hospitality during our stay there. We arranged to meet up with Gogo sometime in Buenos Aires and with Rojo in Guayaquil. But the most significant thing was the affectionate farewell we got at the hospital. Zoraida remembers it thus:

> When it was time for them to move on, we had to organize a new collection just like the first time. The doctors from the hospital, the lab and some from Pesce's department all contributed, buying them a frying pan and sauce pan, since they did their own cooking; I also made them jars of jam, bread and cake to last for at least a couple of days.[36]

---

35 W. Gálvez Rodríguez, Op. cit., p. 243.
36 Ib., p. 244.

Saying goodbye to the patients was a whole different story. Ernesto, with his typical Guevara prudishness about showing his feelings, barely wrote, "The farewell with the patients was more or less emotional, I plan to write."[37] In truth, it was one of the most emotional moments of the trip and speaks to the curing power of solidarity among people. Ernesto had done nothing more than touch them, talk to them, give them his affection, but that had been enough for them to feel that something in their lives could change. Ernesto embraced them and talked to each and every one. They all gave us some little gift, whatever they could—a piece of fruit, a handcraft, a drawing. Everyone's eyes were brimming with tears. No one said goodbye, barely even "see you later". We knew that we would probably never see them again, but our goodbyes were always "see you soon". Overwhelmed by emotion and without thinking about it, I took the hand of one of the patients. And then I couldn't stop and shook hands with them all. It was the first time I had done that.

Once we left and I came back to my senses, I began to worry, "Ernesto, are you sure leprosy isn't contagious? Tell me the truth so I don't touch anything with this hand. "

"No, you idiot, put your hand down—you look like you're flagging down the bus. Leprosy doesn't spread like that; I'm not suicidal either."

Our friend the bullfighter got us cheap tickets on the "bus" to Piura, much like the one that had brought us to Lima. In reality, they were just trucks that pushed the cargo out of the way and put two wooden planks for the "passengers" to sit on. We traveled along the coast,

37 E. Guevara, Otra vez, p. 21.

which is very pretty, but in spite of the intense heat, we weren't able to take a swim because the Pacific at that latitude is freezing. We were already dreaming about the warmth and beaches of Ecuador. Along the way, we again felt the lack of funds at mealtime and when it was time to sleep. Luckily, we had the farewell gifts from Lima. We went back to sleeping in crummy hotels or on the wooden seats of the bus and eating the mysterious stews they served in the town markets when we stopped. They'd serve up a plate of the meal of the day on a plank and give you a spoon. At that point, with our scant finances and all that still lay ahead of us, food was a serious issue. We had to plan it very carefully—it was almost like a blood transfusion. In order to charm people and score a meal from above, we remembered the advice from a Spanish traveler who had explained his technique for begging, which involved following the ideological bent of the potential benefactor. He said that whenever he arrived at a town, he always found out who was Republican and who was Fascist. Adjusting his discourse accordingly, depending on who he was speaking to, he managed to get a handout of a piece of bread, a place to sleep, etc.

As we approached the border with Ecuador, the traditional hatred bred of years of border disputes between Ecuadorians and Peruvians became more accentuated. When we mentioned our destination, the subject inevitably came up. We, of course, were always on the side of the Peruvians, "Well, we don't have any choice but to cross Ecuador, because we're going north, but we're just passing through and don't plan to stay any longer than we have to. We've heard that the people there aren't nearly as nice as Peruvians." And everyone happily shared whatever they could with us.

Going back to the disorganized life and random meals

had horrible effects on Ernesto's asthma. We stopped for a whole day in the Peruvian town of Piura while Ernesto stayed inside trying to recover. That night, he came out for a stroll with me and summed it up in one line: "It's a typical provincial capital like in Argentina, just with more new cars."[38]

The following day we set out for the border town of Tumbes. We "chatted up" the driver and managed to travel for next to nothing. We drove all day, passing through uncountable towns, among which Ernesto mentions in his journal, Talara, "a picturesque oil port."[39] In Tumbes, he had another spell of asthma which kept him shut up in the hotel while I took a walk around. There wasn't much to see. Perú was already in the past and Ecuador awaited us just a few kilometers away. It was there in Tumbes that the Peruvian police stamped our exits in our passports. It was September 27, 1953.

---

38 Ib., p. 21.
39 Ib., p. 21.

CHAPTER 5

Ecuador

Ciudad de Guatemala, enero 5 de 1954
Goldito quetrido: (mitad joda mitad defectos dactilográficos)
        Recien al llegar a esta primaveral ciudad donde nos es-
tamos cagando de frio recibí una carta bidestinada que Calica me mandó
desde Caracas. Hubiera querido escribirte antes pero carecía de medios e-
conómicos para hacerlo, luego de la catastrofe que siguió a la separación
de Calica y antes no lo hacía porque eran noticias comunes.
        Para historiarte el viaje comensaré diciendo que no hubo
en ningún momento bronca con Calica como parecía que creyeran uds. por all
según las preguntas y cuentos de la vieja. Simplemente, dí libertad a mi yo
esplorador y me largué a una aventura que para mi no ofrecía peligros de
ninguna especie, fuera del eventual de la perdida de los haberes monetarios
que para mi no tiene ninguna importancia (te puedo decir esto sin petulancia porque vendí hasta la camisa y me importa un carajo). Para Calica, en
cambio, la cosa era muy diferente y creo que yo no me hubiera separado de
él si frente a una consulta imperiosa para que se definiera por si o por
no, cometido la debilidad de decir si, en un primer momento. A mi se me calen
tó el pico y cuando él ya hechó marcha atrás yo decidí seguir adelante con
los faroles. Evidentemente, hubiera sido una boludez de Calica venir para
estos pagos donde cada mango hay que buscarlo con lupa y donde lo interesante, que son los problemas políticos, económicos y sociales, es de una naturaleza tal que a él le importa un quezo. No se como andará por Caracas,
pues las últimas noticias no eran definitivas en el sentido de empleo pero
tengo la seguridad de que le irá mejor que aquí ya que este es un país muy
pobre y carente en absoluto de industrias que es donde tiene su porvenir
Calica.
        Salimos para Panamá de garrón en un barquito de cabota-

I knew that the moment the great governing spirit strikes the blow to divide all humanity into just two opposing factions, I would be on the side of the common people.

—ERNESTO GUEVARA

In Ecuador, Ernesto finally found what he had been looking for all along without knowing it. His destiny as a globetrotter would begin to make sense and find direction there. He was already dreaming about solutions to the problems he had seen and experienced. In Guayaquil he slowly began the process of transformation from Ernesto into Che. I now know that that was where our destinies began to diverge.

But we knew nothing of this when we crossed the border separating Perú and Ecuador at the town of Aguas Verdes. We had more immediate concerns like avoiding the gangs of thieves teeming close to the bridge we had to cross to get to Huaquillas, the Ecuadorian border post. Like on so many other occasions, once in Ecuadorian territory, the stamping of passports went way beyond the merely procedural—there were the standard objections, all sorts of questions, etc. We weren't tourists, we were young wanderers with little backing in the way of visas or currency. Thus, once again, we answered questions regarding where we were from, where we were going, why, with what money, etc. We also took that Spanish traveler's advice once again, only this time in the opposite way we had done in Perú. To ingratiate ourselves, we mentioned how badly we had been treated there—which wasn't true—and ended up winning over the Ecuadorians that way. They gave us a corner to sleep in and something to eat and drink. "One day lost traveling, which Calica took advantage of to fill up on beer,"[1]

---

1 E. Guevara, *Otra vez,* p. 21.

Ernesto writes, bored, in his journal. He doesn't mention that the beers were many, because he had to abstain due to his asthma which was beginning to flare up again. The heat and mosquitoes let us know that we were in the tropics, although none of this particularly bothered us. They stamped our passports on September 28, 1953.

That same day, we set out to hitch a ride to Santa Marta, since by then we didn't even have enough to cover the modest price of the bus. The financing of our trip from here on to Venezuela was a mystery. What little was left in the chastity belt was negligible. In Santa Marta we took a boat for Guayaquil. It was an old cargo ship with a cranky motor that also took passengers. Far from being a cruise ship, this craft carried no tourists and had no amenities; rather, its main cargo was cattle and above the improvised corral, they hung hammocks for the human passengers. We traveled along the river until Puerto Bolivar; night had already fallen when our precarious craft set out to sea to make its way up the coast. We laughed thinking about what would happen if we fell asleep and tipped out of our hammocks.

"I won't be able to sleep," I assured.

"Cut the crap, Calica. What do you think this is—a cruise ship?"

"But what if I fall on the cows ... "

"Well, you'll get a horn in your rear, that's all," said Ernesto and his contagious laughter worked once again to desired effect. I also started laughing and told myself that the die had been cast, I might as well sleep. Exhaustion, fatigue and acute hunger combined were more powerful than the smell of manure, the mooing and the clatter of hooves on the boat's metal floor. After all, we were at least a little more comfortable than the cows. We slept with one leg hanging out to keep from flipping over.

We woke the next morning as we were approaching Guayaquil. "Me, always with asthma,"[2] remarks Ernesto in his journal entry on the boat trip. A surprise awaited us at the port: As the boat docked, we saw the unmistakable silhouette of El Gordo Rojo, the young lawyer we had met in La Paz and seen in Lima as well. And he wasn't alone—there were three other fellows with him. It was such a pleasure to have someone waiting for us, something that had not happened before then. As we were getting off the boat, we experienced a repeat of the same scene that had occurred at the La Quiaca station. Once again, a guy wanted to help with Ernesto's bag and an argument ensued. Ernesto told him that he didn't have any money for a tip (absolutely true) and the man insisted that his was a regulation service at this port, that he was backed by the union and God knows what else. After several shoves, slaps and in-your-faces in mutual demonstrations of strength, his companions headed our way and things started to look bad. But the presence of the friends who had come to meet us—three of them big guys—convinced them to let us go without further problems. We got off cheaply that time.

After a hug from Rojo, the standard introductions of our small welcome committee were in order: Eduardo "Gualo" García, Andro Herrero and Oscar Valdovinos. They were all law students from the University of La Plata (Argentina) and just as broke as we were. They were held up in Guayaquil waiting for a boat to take them to Panamá, from which point they planned to walk to Guatemala. The only route to Panamá was by sea since the Darién isthmus was impossible to cross by land. The interest Guatemala held was not of a tourist nature—the objective was to get a firsthand view of life

---

2 Ib., p. 21.

under the military-led socialist government of Jacobo Arbenz in a Latin America then dominated by the United States and its local strongmen: Somoza, Trujillo, Batista, Pérez Jiménez and Odría. There, agrarian reform was seriously being put into practice, much beyond what we had seen in the Bolivian reform, still in diapers. In one of the many detailed letters that he wrote to his future wife, Herrero describes meeting us and Rojo in a letter dated October 8, 1953:

> The trio seems to have become a quartet and, for the moment, a sextet. And no, this doesn't mean that, after so long here, we've had babies! What happened was we ran into El Gordo Rojo, a lawyer friend of ours from the Radical Party who took asylum a while ago in the Guatemalan Embassy. We thought that he'd already be there by now. But he went first to Chile and Bolivia, then continued by land to get here, where he ran into the same problem we're having with finding a boat. Needless to say, the night we ran into each other, nobody slept. We went for a chocolate from one of the carts on the boardwalk and stayed up all night, talking the whole time. At eight in the morning we went to wait for two more Argentines that he had befriended in Bolivia and Perú. They're great guys. One of them is a doctor who specializes in leprosy. He's planning to go work in Venezuela at a leper colony on the Orinoco River. His friend is a medical student from Córdoba who's also going there. Of course, they came to the Pensión María Luisa.

The pensión had at one point been a luxurious colonial mansion on the banks of the Guayas River. Now it was a partial ruins, falling to pieces and surrounded by a slum, the Quinta Pareja. The owner had divided the enormous rooms with wooden crates and bamboo wrapped in old newspapers, renting out the subdivisions for a few pesos. You couldn't see your neighbors, but you could hear everything. All six of us crammed the best we could into one of the rooms. Andro describes it in the same letter:

> And our room became a branch of "La Cabaña" [The Cabin] or some student flat in Córdoba: mate and late-night talks, constant joking, absolute community, discussion of future projects, reminiscing about home, lists of mutual friends, etc.—a total riot. We annexed the hall outside the room, where two mattresses were placed and separated from the "living room" by a blanket hung over a wire. Two more mattresses were added on the floor (Gualo García had just arrived from Quito and had no bed). You can imagine what all this was like.

Ernesto defines the nature of the group in his journal: "We formed a sort of closed circle of students with the last rounds of mate we had left. The consul was impervious to our entreaties for a few more leaves of infusion."[3]

Days of searching, companionship and a certain degree of concern about resources for carrying on with the trip ensued. There wasn't much to see in the city. "Guayaquil is, like all ports, a pretext of a city, nearly lifeless on its own, that revolves around the daily event of boats coming or going,"[4] Ernesto writes. We all shared the scarcity, the awful hotel food and debt owed to María Luisa, which grew as the days passed. They made

---

3 Ib., p. 21.
4 Ib., p. 22.

plans to get to Guatemala "adventurously when it came to money,"[5] according to Ernesto, and we concentrated on our hopes for obtaining the means to get to Venezuela with the connection Celia had made in Buenos Aires with President Velasco Ibarra's wife. Ernesto wrote a letter to his father on October 4, describing our situation:

> Dear Pop,
>
> Our journey, slow of course, becomes more and more interesting ... I think we'll be heading out day after tomorrow for Quito, where we plan to take on Tato Velasco or his accomplice ... As for the financial aspect of the trip, there's enough left to get us through and, worse case scenario, Alberto said he'd send whatever we need ... I hope business, partners and funding are all in order and that Mom and other female dead-weights have achieved financial independence! As for us leaving tomorrow or the next day, take that with a grain of salt, because you know me by now. For lack of a definite return date, I'll send a hug for you instead and the two dead-weights as well,
>
> Your son, the Doctor[6, 7]

This letter raises the issue that was becoming more and more of a concern to Ernesto: his sense of wasting time and the impossibility of helping out his family financially. As for asking for help from them, there was no question about that. He lies to his father when he tells him that "there's enough left to get us through" and

---

5 W. Gálvez Rodríguez, Op. cit., p. 245.
6 Ib., p. 245 and 246.
7 Alludes to a play written by Uruguayan playwriter Florencio Sánchez called *M'hijo el dotor* (*My son, the doctor*). Premiered in 1903, it portrays the social aspirations of turn-of-the-century immigrants.

that Alberto would send us whatever we needed, but that was a pact we had made before ever leaving Buenos Aires. And Ernesto kept his word. So did I. In my letters to my mother, I also told the same lies so as not to worry her, because we knew that Dolly and Celia exchanged news about us. With our positive attitudes, we gave the definite impression that either Velasco Ibarra would help us out or Alberto would be in a position to do so. In truth, neither was a sure thing.

I loved the student-community life—it brought back memories and made me feel like I was back in the Barrio Clínicas of my student days. It was a breath of fresh air to be in a democratic country where you didn't see armed military like in Perú. "Here, there's a good atmosphere of personal freedom that contrasts with the suffocating one in Perú," Ernesto wrote to his father. Nevertheless, he was edgy and felt dissatisfied—he was like a volcano on the verge of erupting.

Our interests were leading us in different directions. During the day, I went off with Gualo and Andro Herrero walking around the port, strolling through the little food-stalls where, thanks to our Argentine gift of gab, everyone like us and we managed to get them all to share a little something with us. When we returned at night to the infamous pensión, there were amazing numbers of rats—or *pericos* as they're called in Ecuador—of such a size that I had never before seen. They even seemed to have a different temperament from Argentine rats; one had to walk around them since they were oblivious to our footsteps and continued their eating unperturbed. Not long before, Ecuador had suffered outbreaks of the bubonic plague and you could still see old people with the scar left from the bubo on their forehead.

I got along very well with Gualo and even more so when I discovered in conversation that he was the brother of the famous "Chivo" García, head of the FUC, the University of Córdoba Federation in which I had represented my class. Ernesto, on the other hand, teamed up with Valdovinos and Rojo and they made incursions into political and literary circles. "Poets around here are an industry," he would say in reference to the numerous writers he knew. Hilda Gadea, his first wife, speaks of the cultural climate in which he moved in her book, *Años decisivos*:

> In Ecuador, Ernesto met many communist youth leaders as well as intellectuals, including Jorge Icaza, with whom he talked at length about the peasant problem and who would dedicate his book *Huasipungo* to Ernesto; Guevara later gave the book to me as gift.[8]

In his journal Ernesto mentions Jorge Maldonado Reinella and Fortunato Safadi "psychiatrist and *bolche*[9], like his friend Maldonado."[10] Through them he met the few leprosy specialists in the city. "They have a recluse house with thirteen people living in pretty bad conditions and with little specific treatment. The hospitals are at least clean and not entirely bad."[11] Safadi also took him to see some places along the coast that "were like any rainy area with flood-prone rivers."[12] It was a place like our Delta del Tigre. The rest of the day he would spend playing chess with the other guys in the pensión and talking politics, something that was becoming

---

8 Hilda Gadea, *Che Guevara. Años decisivos*, México DF, Aguilar, 1978.
9 Bolshevik.
10 E. Guevara, *Otra vez*, p. 22.
11 Ib., p. 22.
12 Ib., p. 22.

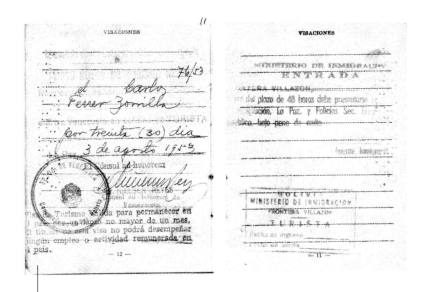

Our passage into Ecuador via Huanquillas on Sept. 28th and the visa for Guatemala obtained in Guayaquil. The change of route from Venezuela to Guatemala was fundamental in shaping the future Che. I got the visa when I planned to go with Ernesto to that country, but later changed my mind and continued on to Caracas.

increasingly more interesting to him. One of Herrero's letters gives an idea of the tone of those conversations:

Guevara, the doctor, is a very interesting guy. Last year he sailed down the Amazon on a raft. We chatted at length about the unbelievable problems these people have, practically unknown to people there. It's really irritating to see all this, even more so when you think of the insensitivity of all these feudal, reactionary oligarchies and the greed of imperialist groups. And then when one recalls that even the intelligent, quite politicized fellows over there in the FUA, despite its reputation, claim that imperialism is not a problem in Latin America and that this type of penetration is progressive in purpose—it makes you want to start shooting.

—a large truth that we began to clearly see.

In the middle of such dire straits, Gualo got us invited to a dance hosted by the FEUE (University Federation of Ecuador), where they were going to choose the student queen. Just to do something and see if we could score some food and beverages, maybe a girl or two (which Andro did *not* mention in his detailed letter to his girlfriend), we all went except Valdo, because he didn't have a dark suit and refused to be seen without evening attire. This caused a lot of joking, because the rest of us by that time couldn't have cared less about the way we dressed. Ernesto even less. The party in fact did serve to curb our hunger and entertain us with the ridiculous evening gowns worn by the queens "dancing all high and mighty in their royal cliques," as described by Andro in one of his letters. Translated, this meant they wouldn't even give us the time of day.

Rojo and Valdovinos procured a place on a boat for Panamá once they had paid 35 dollars and knocked on the door of every "contact" El Gordo had in the city. With the departure of two members of the group, what we longed for and what we lacked became more apparent. Mainly we missed El Gordo, always happy, free of money troubles—unlike the rest of us, he never wanted for cash. Andro describes the general sentiment to his girlfriend:

> Saturday was the departure day. We almost got emotional over it … El Gordo left us an overcoat and a gold ring to cash in. But mainly, it seems that his lucky star—for sure, he's a lucky guy—came along to break our bad spell. Not to mention, you can imagine how meeting up with him really lifted our spirits. He's a happy, good-natured guy and we have a lot in common.

Contrary to what we expected, they disappeared altogether without a letter, a telegram or any word whatsoever.

In this mood, a joke ended up changing the course of our trip, Ernesto's life and possibly history. Ernesto describes it to his mother this way:

> We walked along a bit, missing home, Calica, García (one of our acquisitions) and I. We talked about how great it was that two of the group had been able to get passage to Panamá ... So García, just joking, suddenly invited us to go with them to Guatemala and I was in a unique mental state to accept. Calica promised to give his answer the following day, which also ended up being affirmative, such that there were now four new candidates for Yankee opprobrium.[13]

In his journal he writes: "This all came about as the result of a joke made by García .... The idea was already there latent—it just needed that little extra push for me to decide. Calica follows me."[14] Andro also mentions the news in this letter dated October 8th:

> Guevara and Carlos have decided to come with us to Guatemala before heading to Venezuela. It all started as a joke, but is now serious. El Gordo and Valdo are going to flip when they see all four of us show up. Of course, it's not a sure thing that we'll all be able to get passage together, but we'll try.

But getting to Guatemala was no simple task—we had to find a way to get there with our pockets nearly empty

---

13 W. Gálvez Rodríguez, Op. cit., p. 246 and 247.
14 E. Guevara, *Otra vez*, p. 22.

(the chastity belt, I won't even mention anymore because at that point, what it held was so negligible it wasn't worth worrying over); the mandatory entry and exit visa for Panamá, which we had to cross to get to Guatemala; and cash to pay off the hotel debt. It was just then that we learned that Velasco Ibarra was coming on official visit to Guayaquil to cut the ribbon on some important works— we thought we had found our life raft.

"Don't worry about a thing," we told Gualo and Andro, "we've got the solution for getting out of here. We're taking our letter of recommendation to go see Velasco and ask him to find us a spot on one of their official planes or boats headed for Panama." We took it as a *fija*[15].

We ironed our best clothes, shined our shoes and I even went to have my beard shaved off. I had to bargain the price of the shave with the barber, who wanted to charge me extra for the uncommon length of it. So, looking the best we could, we went to the hotel where the President and his entourage were staying and requested a meeting. After a long wait, his Chief of Protocol received us, one Mr. Anderson, whom it befell to hear out our pathetic requests. He was a young man of insignificant stature, very pompous, all decked out in a strikingly neat military uniform. We listed our financial woes in exaggerated detail, but he cut us off to inquire about the person who had recommended us, the first lady's friend, whom he also knew. This was when the stumbling began. To each specific question about this woman, we gave vague replies that revealed the truth of it: that we had barely spoken with her by phone and we didn't recall the details of her life in Buenos Aires that Celia had told us about.

"And how are her children?"

---

15 Sure thing.

"Really well … growing up," we improvised without knowing whether she even had children. Ernesto tried to change the subject to get out of the swamp we were sinking in. "We can speak frankly with you, sir, since this is a democratic government."

"Why, of course," the ceremonious Chief of Protocol said.

"What we want is to get to Guatemala and get a close-up view of the popular movement underway there."

"I see … ," assented Anderson.

"We don't mind traveling with cows—we already have experience—we have no pretensions, if you could see fit to give us a place on any government boat or plane to Guatemala or to Panamá, where we can continue by land."

"I'm sorry, but that is impossible," he affirmed dryly.

"Or any other type of help would be welcome," in desperation, Ernesto took a shot in the dark for whatever he could get.

"Look, boys, I'll tell you how it is. Life is full of ups and downs and you guys are in a "down"—don't worry, better times will come. Now, if you'll excuse me, I'm in an "up" and must go to the firefighter's ceremony. It's been a pleasure, eh?"

He got up and left without offering "even a drink—not one little drink to drown our sorrows in … ,"[16] Ernesto describes with irony to Celia.

Gualo and Herrero were anxiously waiting for us at the door of the other "hotel", the María Luisa in Quinta Pareja. We had to come clean: operation handout had failed miserably. We suspected that our sincerity with the democratic official had been excessive. Ecuador was

---

16 Jon Lee Anderson, *Che. Una vida revolucionaria*, Buenos Aires, Emecé, 1997, p. 125.

a democracy surrounded by dictatorships and moved with extreme caution to avoid offending anyone. It surely did not seem a very good idea to send four possible guerrilla fighters to Panamá on official government transport. So we had to move to Plan B; too bad there was no Plan B ... or C or D, for that matter. Just like always on that trip, we would have to improvise.

"Plans undone and redone, economic distress and Guayaquilean phobias," Ernesto summed up our activities and sentiments on the following days in his journal. The situation was this: We estimated the expenses for the trip at about 200 dollars. We pooled what little we all had left (Andro observes parenthetically in one of his letters that "they [us] have more than we do") and it came to a grand total of 120.80 pesos. To make up the difference, we set out to *pinchinchear*[17] everything we had that wasn't absolutely necessary. Herrero made a list in one of his letters: "The ring El Gordo left us to use in a pinch, his overcoat, the books, one of Carlos' coats, my raincoat, etc., etc. The camera [Ernesto's] we're keeping as a last resort."

Ernesto, with his dry wit, also tells his mother of our days as small businessmen: "Your suit, your masterpiece, that jewel of your dreams, has died a heroic death in a pawn shop, just like everything else that wasn't necessary in my luggage, leaving me with a much lighter load in exchange for economic (sigh of relief) stability."[18] Stretching his creativity, Ernesto had the idea that we could use the pooled funds to buy a small boat and sail up the coast to Panamá. This surprised me, but since I was always lacking a plan and the idea came from Ernesto, I considered it nearly possible and backed him

---

17 Pawn off.
18 W. Gálvez Rodríguez, Op. cit., p. 247.

up. However, Andro and Gualo had a laughing fit, thinking it was a joke (they still didn't know him).

"I'm not kidding—it can be done," insisted Ernesto stubbornly as the others tried to explain how sailing on the open sea was technically impossible in a little rowboat without know-how. (Three years later in 1956, Ernesto would prove that everything was possible: A modest craft, the Granma, would cross the Gulf of Mexico to Cuba with a load four times its maximum cargo, surviving storms, mechanical problems and lack of supplies. After seven days of turbulent navigating, the crew—members of the July 26th liberation movement—would put ashore on Cuban territory. One of them would be Ernesto Guevara, already Che by then. With his typical wit, he would later say, "It was more like a shipwreck than putting ashore.")

A more concrete alternative emerged: We would convince one of the numerous cargo ship captains to bring us aboard for a few pesos and ask him to co-sign before the Panamanian authorities to get our visas. In exchange, we would work on board. It wasn't easy and we grew tired of walking the docks. "In Panama, days of scarcity await us; what we need to know is if Panamá awaits us ... ,"[19] Ernesto comments during those days of uncertainty.

Gualo and I went to talk to the captain of one ship, the Guayos, scheduled to sail on October 18th for Panama. He was a great guy and practically gave his word that he'd take all four of us, but at the last minute he informed us that he couldn't, because the company wouldn't permit us aboard without a visa for Panamá and a pre-purchased ticket for Guatemala. Once again, frustration and the sense of being trapped with no way

---

19 E. Guevara, *Otra vez*, p. 22.

out and meanwhile, our debts were piling up.

In this situation, one event changed the course of my personal history. One of those afternoons, with nothing better to do than roam around the port looking for a way out, I was invited to play a pick-up game of soccer. I've already mentioned the reputation we Argentines have for soccer. When the game was over, one of the Ecuadorian guys came up to me.

"Hey, you play really well. Wouldn't you like to come try out for a team in Quito?"

"I don't know, I don't even have the money for the trip and I'm with a friend ... ," I said skeptically.

"Well, bring your friend along. And don't worry about the trip—we're headed there in a couple of days and I have a cargo truck that I make my living with. In Quito, the club will pay for room and board plus your salary."

It was a tempting offer that I kept mulling over. In Guayaquil, things were becoming increasing unbearable. If the hotel cost 100 pesos, we were paying 20 and the rest was accumulating on the bill. Rojo and Valdovinos had not written again and seemed to have left us to our own devices. The visa for Panamá was impossible to obtain and the ship captains wouldn't risk taking us without all the paperwork in order. The dream of Venezuela seemed to be further and further away. Going to Quito for free and getting paid for playing soccer on top of that was like a dream come true.

I tried to convince Ernesto, but with no luck—he wanted to go to Guatemala and saw all the roadblocks as surmountable obstacles.

"Look, we're held up here and nearly out of cash. We've heard nothing from El Gordo and Valdo and there's no boat for us. We're going to end up stuck here forever."

"Something will turn up," Ernesto insisted.

Goldito quetrido: (mitad joda mitad defectos dactilográficos)

Recien al llegar a esta primaveral ciudad donde nos estamos cagando de frío recibí una carta bidestinada que Calica me mandó desde Caracas. Hubiera querido escribirte antes pero carecía de medios económicos para hacerlo, luego de la catastrofe que siguió a la separación de Calica y antes no lo hacía porque eran noticias comunes.

Para historiarte el viaje comensaré diciendo que no hubo en ningún momento bronca con Calica como parecía que creyeran uds. por ahí según las preguntas y cuentos de la vieja. Simplemente, dí libertad a mi yo explorador y me largué a una aventura que para mi no ofrecía peligros de ninguna especie, fuera del eventual de la perdida de los haberes monetarios que para mi no tiene ninguna importancia (te puedo decir esto sin petulancia porque vendí hasta la camisa y me importa un carajo). Para Calica, en cambio, la cosa era muy diferente y creo que yo no me hubiera separado de él si frente a una consulta imperiosa para que se definiera por si o por no, cometido la debilidad de decir si, en un primer momento. A mi se me calentó el pico y cuando él ya hecho marcha atrás yo decidí seguir adelante con los faroles. Evidentemente, hubiera sido una boludez de Calica venir para estos pagos donde cada mango hay que buscarlo con lupa y donde lo interesante, que son los problemas políticos, económicos y sociales, es de una naturaleza tal que a él le importa un quezo. No se como andará por Caracas, pues las últimas noticias no eran definitivas en el sentido de empleo pero tengo la seguridad de que le irá mejor que aquí ya que este es un país muy pobre y carente en absoluto de industrias que es donde tiene su porvenir Calica.

Salimos para Panamá de garrón en un barquito de cabotaje uno de cuyos dueños era un italiano que se sentía argentino y nos trató en forma magnífica. Llegamos sin un cobre a la ciudad y tuvimos que hacer de todo para conseguir mangos. Ahí deje todos mis libros y lo que me quedaba de ropa y me fuí con un muchacho García, tirando dedo hasta Costa Rica donde nos trataron muy bien. Seguimos enese mismo tren para el Norte, pero al llegar a la frontera con Nicaragua nos encontramos con un grupo de argentinos que iban en sentido contrario en un automovil y estaban varados por las condiciones intransitables del camino. Ellos nos trajeron hasta la ciudad de Guatemala donde llegamos el día 24 de diciembre, justo a tiempo para pasar la navidad en familia.

Las perspectivas no son extremadamente alagüeñas ya que los tramites administrativos para conseguir empleo de médico en Sanidad dependiente del gobierno son muy largos y la profesión no se puede ejercer libremente sino que hay que seguir un curso para incorporarse al cuerpo médico, lo que tarda bastante. Por ahora tiro con unas traducciones que hago en colaboración con la mujer de un amigo mío, ella pone el inglés y yo el castellano; se come. Tal vez empiese a trabajar como tecnico de algún alergista que haya en la ciudad pero está condicionado a la docilidad de los tipos para dejarse dirigir (toma mierda). En Panamá me mande una conferencia sobre alergia en la universidad a la que fueron veinte tipos, pero entre ellos Pi Suñer que estuvo de acuerdo con los lineamientos generales y me felicito muy calurosamente. En este mes decidiré que hago, si me quedo los dos años que en un principio había pensado o solamente seis meses, para conocer esto y juntar algún peso para organizar la huida a otro país más "dolarisado", en cuyo caso daría con mis huesos en Venezuela previa una visita que Alberto Granado tiene que hacerme por aquí.

Espero que hayan pasado las fiestas de fin de año con las tradicionales broncas familiares quese arman para estos eventos y que vos hayas puteado a Dios y Maria Santísima por todos esos problemas insolubles que se te presentan. Me imagino que andarás con una ristra de materias colgadas y con el pelo en franca decadencia. Me enteré que al payuca se le dieron con queso (y a Guachito?). Un fuerte abrazo para tu familia y otro

---

This letter is of extreme value to me. I read it only a few years ago. In it, Ernesto tells my brother a few months after our separation what the reasons were behind our taking different paths. You can see the figure of Che emerging here already.

"Come on, if we don't like it, we come back—anyway, it's free, we don't have to spend a cent."

"You go and see what the deal is in Quito, then write me. If we don't find a boat, I'll follow you. Or we'll meet up later—we just need to keep in touch."

Over the days I spent trying to decide, several potential boats appeared, but ended up turning us down. I was torn; on one hand, I wanted to continue on with Ernesto and our new friends and not give up that fraternity we had formed. But then I thought of the purpose of my trip: to work and be able to help out my family in Buenos Aires, my mother a widow and my two brothers studying medicine. I felt I had a moral debt with them. I planned to get a job in Venezuela, maybe even take a real leap, snagging the daughter of one of those oil tycoons. (I didn't know the oil was state-owned.) Venezuela symbolized this possibility.

The trip to Guatemala, however, meant following the path of adventure. Ernesto also had his doubts, but in his case, he didn't care about the financial aspect of it; he was more concerned about not having any word from Rojo and Valdovinos and being stuck in Guayaquil. I was terrified of being trapped and tried to talk him into coming with me. There was no convincing him. I finally decided to try my luck alone in Quito, thinking that I'd meet up with Ernesto soon after. It was nothing definite for either of us; the idea was we'd see each other soon in Quito or a bit further on. Ernesto tells his mother about my decision in a letter from Guayaquil dated October 21, 1953:

But that was the moment when all our bad luck in the consulates started, crying every day for them to give us a visa for Panamá, the requirement we're lacking, and after numerous alternative plans with their subsequent psychological ups and downs, [Calica] appears to have decided to back out.[20]

We split up our luggage, which by that point was completely mixed up since we were sharing what few items of clothing had survived being pawned for a few pesos. We also had an enormous package full of film rolls wrapped in lead paper. They were all the photos of the trip we hadn't had enough to pay to have developed. Neither one of us wanted to carry that package–the possibility of developing even one of those rolls seemed very remote. After much back and forth, Ernesto agreed to keep them.

"Maybe I'll be back in a few days; don't make me carry that ton of lead," I said to him. (Over the years, those photos never turned up; most likely they were forgotten in some hotel, left in a truck bed or very possibly lost when his and Gualo's boat sunk when they got to Guatemala. I was never able to get over the loss of all those photographic mementos. The few photos I still have of that trip, published for the first time in this book, are those that I sent my mother by letter.)

"Look, I'll send you a telegram. If the boat doesn't come within two or three days, a week at the most, I'll go on with you."

That was how I said goodbye to Ernesto, with no drama. In his journal, he noted, "Calica left for Quito in a private truck for free."[21] The trip from Guayaquil to Quito lasted three days, because we were partying-drinking, women ... all in a beautiful landscape. Meanwhile, Ernesto and the others were still working on getting passage to Panamá.

---

20 W. Gálvez Rodríguez, Op. cit., p. 247.
21 E. Guevara, *Otra vez*, p. 23.

Monday we tried again, this time with a transit order for 35 dollars in Garcia's and my names, since we had resolved to leave first; the result was negative. With this latest news, we took our last shot and sent a telegram to Calica for him to wait for us.[22]

Things were going well for me: The trip had been fun and didn't cost a cent thanks to my new Ecuadorian friends, and I had an easy "job" waiting for me in Quito so I could save a little money. Ernesto's telegram announcing that he was on his way was all I needed to make my happiness complete. However, there was other news waiting for me in the consulate that wasn't nearly so pleasant.

"Come in, take a seat—I have something to tell you," the consul invited me in, poker-faced. I nearly fell over from fear—such affability was confusing.

"What's wrong?" I asked excitedly.

"It's a very serious matter."

I thought of my mother, Celia, my brothers, our families. I asked in fear, "Bad news from Buenos Aires?" Silence.

"See this son-of-a-bitch Indian—see him?" he said, pointing to the little Colla who had shown me in and who had remained in the corner with his head bowed. "I asked him to remove the stamps from the envelopes with the heat of a candle—I collect stamps—and the savage brought me the stamps, but he burned the letters— all your letters. I'm sorry." I was speechless; for me this was a real blow, because it meant losing contact with our families, with the girlfriends we'd left behind in Buenos Aires who continued writing to us. I cursed my bad luck, although I later suspected that the story of the

---

22 Ib., p. 23.

Indian was a lie and that the truth was they had fingered us after the conversation with Anderson and gone through our mail. The only thing that kept my spirits up was re-reading Ernesto's telegram that read: "Wait for me. I'm coming with you."

Meanwhile, in Guayaquil things were back on track:

> Last night I had a meeting with Enrique Arbuiza, the insurance agent who told us that perhaps he could get it and the next morning (today), we spoke with the person in charge at a travel agency who refused as well; however, he gave us another alternative, explaining that the company that would take us to Panamá could provide the letter. The insurance agent was also a friend of the captain of the Guayos and consequently took me to him to explain the problem. The captain initially flinched like he'd burnt his hand on hot milk, but after we clarified things a bit, he calmed down and agreed to give us his final decision this afternoon. Anyway, we sent a new telegram to Quito to let Calica know the latest, so he'll be going it alone now, at least until Bogotá ... Our plan is to wait for the final word and then two of us will go to Panamá or set sail all three of us as soon as possible. We'll see.[23]

The telegram hit me like a bomb the next day: "Our ship came in. We board as soon as they load it." Suddenly, I realized I was all alone, that the decision that my youth had allowed me to so lightly make had consequences. There I was, thousands of kilometers away from home without a cent to my name, completely alone.

---

23 Ib., p. 23.

Over the years, I began to understand the force of destiny. Maybe the world wouldn't have had Che if that ship hadn't come in and he had come with me to Caracas instead. Ours weren't two different geographical destinies; they were two different life choices. One was a great political destiny and the other a life of work that included socializing and (material) comforts ... the sirens' song of this shitty world that we live in and find so indispensable.

At that time, things were not so clear to me, but they were to Ernesto. It wasn't until many years later (I had already turned 70) that my brother, El Gordo Ferrer, gave me a letter that Ernesto had sent him from Guatemala dated January 5, 1954 (a few months after our separation), in which he lucidly describes the paths chosen by each of us and why. The contents, published for the first time, are as follows:

Dear Goldito [intentional spelling error],

Upon arrival in this springtime city where we're freezing to death, I received a letter meant for the two of us that Calica forwarded from Caracas. I would have written you before, but didn't have the financial means to do so after the catastrophe that followed my separation from Calica, and before that I didn't because it would have been common news. To fill you in on the trip, I'll start out by saying that there wasn't any fight with Calica as it seems you all believed according to my old lady's questions and comments. It was simply that I freed my inner explorer and took off on an adventure that, for me, didn't pose any type of danger aside from the eventual loss of monetary means, which for me doesn't matter in the least (I say this with no petulance whatsoever—I even sold the shirt on my back and couldn't care less about it). For Calica, though, things were different and I think that I would never have split from him if, when faced with the imperious question of giving a definite "yes" or "no" answer, he hadn't made the mistake of saying "yes" at first. I got excited and when he decided to back out, I chose to continue on into the tunnel. Obviously, it would have been sheer idiocy for Calica to come here, where you have to struggle for every dime; what's interesting— the political, social and economic problems—aren't things that he puts much stock in. I don't know how things are going for him in Caracas, since the last I heard wasn't definite in terms of employment, but I've no doubt that he's better off than he'd be here, since this is a very poor country with absolutely no industry, which is where Calica's future lies.

When I read this letter many years later, the memory of my friend moved me. I appreciated the firmness of his decision to seek his destiny. I regretted not having understood that at the time. Maybe I would have continued on with him. I didn't know that I was separating from Ernesto forever. I also understood how much our separation hurt him, although, always a Guevara, he never expressed it to me.

It was difficult for Ernesto to get out of Ecuador. The captain of the ship that had agreed to take them that day he sent me the last telegram backed out and they had to keep waiting. The bill at the pensión had reached insurmountable proportions and they could find no solution other than *cantar la tosca*[24]. Finally, Andro decided to stay behind as "collateral" to take care of the outstanding debts. Ernesto and Gualo left on October 31, 1953. Andro details the state of their debts in a letter: ·

----

24 Running out on the bill.

I'm all alone. Lonely and taciturn like the sea, as the poem goes. The boys set out in a finale that was tighter than the final lap at the races. Just a few hours before the boat was to leave, we didn't have the money and suspected that they weren't going to get away from the pensión without paying. At the last minute, Monasterio, the Venezuelan, managed to come up with 500 sucres that we used to convince María Luisa to let the boys go. And they set sail. I stayed behind in charge of the debts. Our current situation [in sucres]: *Debts*: 450 to María Luisa, after paying 400 obtained through sale of camera; 540 to Orangel Monasterio for the check he signed to loan the money for the "aces" to leave; 250 to Don Espiridión González for supplies of milk, cigarettes, soap, toothpaste, paper, etc., etc.; 270 to Don Pepe Castro of 'El Sol' from pawn tickets for Guevara and García suits; 130 to the guy in the kiosk for García's debts; 1 to Ayala, the shoeshine-boy (0.60 for the shine, 0.40 for the bus). I don't include the bills I can't pay. *Assets*: 235 cash left from pawning suits; one gold ring, Bolivian engraving, difficult to sell, can offer 250; 200 owed by camera buyer, payable as of Saturday; 10 postage stamps worth 0.80 each for international exchange. As you can see, the matter is a bit unbalanced.

Although they had planned for Andro to take the next ship and catch up with them, he wasn't able to and never saw Ernesto again. With a good dose of humor Andro says: "I've ended up with more *muertos*[25] than Chacarita cemetery."

As for Ernesto, he himself tells my brother Jorge in his

---

25 Literally "dead", used here as slang for "debts".

letter how the trip continued without his sidekick, Calica:

We headed for Panamá for next to nothing in a little trading boat, one of whose owners was an Italian who felt Argentine and was incredibly nice to us. We got to the city without a cent to our names and had to do just about anything for a couple of bucks. There I left all my books and what clothes I had left and set out with this guy [Gualo] García hitching up to Costa Rica, where we were treated really well. We continued on that same northbound train, but when we got to the border with Nicaragua, we met a group of Argentines headed in the opposite direction by car who had been held up by the bad road conditions. They brought us to Guatemala City, where we arrived on December 24th. Just in time to spend the holidays with the family.

The prospects here are nothing to brag about, since the paperwork to get a government job as a doctor in the Health Dept. is tedious and you can't just practice freely here without going through the proper channels to become part of the medical corps, which takes a long time. For the moment, I'm scraping by with some translation work I do with the wife of a friend—she does the English and I do the Spanish; it covers the food. I might start working as a technician for some allergy clinic around here, but that depends upon how open they are to taking orders (eat shit). In Panamá I gave a talk on allergies at the university to an audience of twenty, which included Pi Suñer, who agreed with me along general lines and warmly congratulated me. This month I'll decide what I'm going to do—whether I stay two years as initially planned or just six months to get to know this place and save a few bucks for my next escape to another "dollarized" country, in which case I'd lay my bones in Venezuela, pending a visit from Alberto Granado to see me here.

I hope you've had a good holiday with all the traditional family fights one enjoys at these events and that you've cursed God and the Virgin Mary for all those unsolvable problems that you have. I imagine you've got a string of classes still to pass and a head of hair out of control. I heard that they flunked the *payuca*[26] [Mario Roberto Saravia, a cousin of Ernesto's who at that time was living with the Guevaras and studying medicine]. (What about Chachito [the youngest of the Ferrers, also a medical student]?)

A big hug for your family and another for you—your friend,

Chancho

Write to me at the Argentine consulate where I get all my mail.

As for me, there wasn't anything left for me to do in Ecuador—not even the promise of a job on the soccer team interested me. The only thing I wanted to do was get to Venezuela quickly and get on with the rest of my life. I only had to thumb cross Colombia, a country where a guerrilla movement called *bandolerismo* was in the making. These were merely details for me. Without Ernesto, my experienced companion, without my friend who made everything seem possible, the adventure was over.

---

26 Country boy.

EPILOGUE

Life isn't what one lived, but what one remembers and how one remembers it to tell it.

—GABRIEL GARCÍA MÁRQUEZ

The idea for this book was something that came about little by little over time. For many years, the significance of the figure of Che Guevara—waved about in my face just like the rest of the world's—made me feel that my experience alongside him had been a privilege, but that my words had little to add to the legacy my friend Ernesto had left for humanity. Three years ago Pacho O'Donnell contacted me about an interview for a biography he was writing on Che. Until then, I had been reluctant to tell my story, having seen all the different ways Ernesto's figure had been exploited and how many lies sustained as historical fact. Nevertheless, my conversations with Pacho led me to overcome my initial hesitation. Once we had reached a certain degree of trust, he told me quite seriously, "It is your moral and historical obligation to tell your story. You were the only one who shared everything with him those last months prior to his transformation into Che." That conversation made me understand that what was truest to my friend's way of thinking was to share that privilege that life had granted me; that little slice of Ernesto's life was not only mine, but rather should belong to all those who admire him and seriously study his legacy.

The story told in this book I lived only once, but I was to rediscover it many times in recalling the exploits of my childhood friend. It was 52 years ago in October of 1953 that I saw Ernesto for the last time. We said good-bye with simple *chau* and a brief embrace, like always, like we would see each other again any day. At that moment, without knowing it, I lost my companion in adventure, in travel, in life. In exchange I earned a friend who, in some form or other, has always been with me as an example of moral integrity, as a living lesson in solidarity, in revolutionary commitment.

My life went on like that of most people. I worked, lived in different countries, got married, had two children, endured dictatorships and conditional democracies. But the figure of Ernesto, little by little replaced by that of Che, was always present for me. Not even the science of disinformation orchestrated by the powers-that-be has been able to douse the light that radiates from the image of Comandante Che Guevara—my friend Ernesto.

After the trip he and I shared, I lived for several years in Venezuela. At first, as the reader will have guessed, things were not as easy as I, so oblivious and carefree, had imagined at the time. Fortunately, I had my two guardian angels: Margarita Calvento, who gave me a place to stay in her home and was like a mother to me; and Alberto Granado, who became my good friend and filled part of the vacuum left by Ernesto. Margarita, an Argentine social worker who had lived for years in Venezuela, had helped Ernesto and Alberto during their first trip. Just as she later did with me, she had given them food, advice and all the connections she could. Thanks to her good works, Alberto had landed a job as a biochemist in the Cabo Blanco leper colony at La Guaira and was able to establish himself in Venezuela.

It took me months to find a decently paid job. Meanwhile, I lived at Margarita's house and spent the weekends at the leper colony with Alberto. At our first meeting, he took me to eat lobster and Chilean wine. I thought, "This guy's rolling in it." (Much later on he confessed that he was only trying to impress me. Well, he certainly did that—but it didn't come cheaply!) We talked until the wee hours, I told him of our journey and Ernesto's decision to change course. "That Pelao [Ernesto's nickname]! Now he's changing plans on me and we were going to Paris," he said. For Alberto as well as for me, our dreams of traveling to Europe or taking a boat down the Orinoco vanished without the presence of Ernesto. For a while, we expected him to show up any time. We received updates from him, Alberto helped as best he could and we dreamed of a reunion. In one letter, written December 13, 1953, from Costa Rica to Zoraida Boluarte—our Peruvian benefactress—he recounts the state of things:

> Señora Peirano [the nurse whose house we stayed at in Lima] will surely have told you about the change of course by now. I separated from Calica Ferrer, who is now working in Caracas ... I arrived here by land. I'm still headed to Guatemala, where I plan to be by January. This is my life ... Alberto Granado has already saved a respectable amount of US dollars and is going to Argentina in a few days and then, if he can, on to the United States, then to Mexico, Guatemala, etc. to meet up with me there in three or four months.[1]

Once in Guatemala, he writes in his journal: "Today's positive event was the arrival of a kilo of mate leaves, in addition to a letter from Alberto and Calica telling me of money, which allows me to dream about it for a while."[2]

---

1 W. Gálvez Rodríguez, Op. cit., p. 257.
2 E. Guevara, *Otra vez*, p. 42.

To his adored Aunt Beatriz, in a letter dated February 12, 1954, he speaks of the possibility of going to Venezuela:

> The other idea … is to go to Venezuela for a while with … Granado, subject to a series of prior events that are too many to go into, but would nevertheless not happen before spending the necessary six months in Guatemala, the country that is today the most interesting in America and that must be defended with whatever means.[3]

In the same letter, he mentions being happy that I'd found work in Venezuela, although he sarcastically adds "for a salary not worth writing home about."[4] In June of that same year, still in Guatemala, he writes to Zoraida again with news about us:

> Of my companions, I can tell you that Alberto went on a spree in Argentina and is loaded with cash, and now he plans to go to Europe and take his parents, both Spaniards; and Calica's working as a medical supply salesman earning US$300 per month. As you can see, I'm the only one who's off track, but then again, I'm not working, which is something itself.[5]

News also circulated through the Dolly-Celia connection, since my mother transmitted what Celia told her about her son.

Once Ernesto went underground in Mexico, I no longer had any news of him. One day, El Petiso [Granado] arrived with a copy of the *Universal* and a crazy look in his eyes, "Look! A photo of El Pelao!" And there he was, one of the

---

3 W. Gálvez Rodríguez, Op. cit., p. 274.
4 Ib., p. 275.
5 Ib., p. 299.

detainees accused of plotting to invade Cuba from Mexico. He figured as "an Argentine doctor". Aside from the logical concern I felt for my friend, what occurred to me at that moment was that Ernesto had finally found what he'd been looking for. He was already Che.

The years passed and one day—the Cuban revolution had already triumphed and Ernesto was working for the new government—Alberto announced that he was going to Cuba. He was married to a Venezuelan girl by then and they had two children. He traveled to La Habana alone the first time to see the Revolution firsthand and returned to Caracas with the firm decision to start a new life with his family in Cuba.

"Calica, Ernesto says if you want, the doors are wide open to you, but that you should know that soon Cuba will declare itself a socialist republic and break all ties with the capitalist world," Granado told me and handed me a frogskin wallet that Ernesto had sent as a gift for me (and that I still keep as a memento). Once again, the crossroads, just like in Guayaquil. And once again I felt torn between the part of me that wanted to follow Ernesto and the other that resisted giving up the comfortable life I had in Venezuela, which I now considered my second homeland. Furthermore, Granado's leaving for Cuba would leave me yet again without a bosom friend. But I was living well in Caracas, earning good money—I had a car, lots of good times and was able to send money home to my mother for my brothers to continue their studies. I hesitated—going to Cuba would have been a huge blow to my entire family. And on top of all this, I was in my element, aside from the ups and downs that come of "slow horses and fast women": I loved the races, playing 5-and-6[6], the girls, the booze,

---

6 A popular gambling game in Venezuela at that time.

the nightlife—everything the revolution reproached. I decided to wait a while; "I'm still young—maybe in a few years," I told myself and thus the years went by.

In 1967 when I learned of Ernesto's death, it was a terrible blow. At first, I refused to believe it. I looked at the picture and said, "No, no, no—it's not him." He was so beaten up, so thin and pale, that he looked like another person. I couldn't understand why Ernesto had taken his guerrilla war to the Bolivian peasantry. During our trip, we had gotten to know the indigenous Bolivians that worked the countryside and we knew how difficult it was to get through to them. Aside from the language barrier, the worst thing was breaking that resignation they had to a life of disgrace that had accompanied them for centuries. But Ernesto was used to defying the odds. Until this day, it's hard for me to accept his death. It consoles me to read the moving letter he left for his children, in which his faith in the future for them shines through. He imagined them growing up and reaping the benefits of the Revolution—a revolution that he helped to build, but, always true to his style, rejected its fruits himself. The future he dreamed of became reality for Hilda, Aleida, Camilo, Celia and Ernesto, even though he didn't live to see it. In that letter written in 1965, which was published and I read with so much emotion, he tells them:

> Your father has been a man who acts as he thinks and, for sure, has been true to his convictions. Grow up as good revolutionaries. Study a lot so you'll learn the technique of how to dominate nature. Remember that the revolution is what's important and that each one of us alone is worth nothing. Above all, always be able to sense deep-down any injustice committed against anyone anywhere in the world. This is the

most beautiful quality in a revolutionary.[7]

In my two trips to Cuba I had the opportunity to meet his children personally and confirm that they had heeded well his advice. They all welcomed me with much affection, as did his wife, Aleida. My first trip there was in 1990. I was invited by Froilán González and Adys Cupull, two Cuban writers who had interviewed me in Argentina for the Editora Política [Political Publishing House]. That trip helped to give new meaning to everything I went through with Ernesto. I had always admired the Revolution and the heroic Cuban people for their endurance of 40 years of embargo and who today offer the world culture, sports, world-class healthcare and a unique example of human dignity. But seeing what the Revolution has achieved firsthand, and how even the poorest of Cubans live, made me feel even prouder of my friend Ernesto. The visit also gave me the chance to be reunited with another dear friend: Alberto Granado and his family. Wherever I went, everyone welcomed me and honored me as if I were someone special just for having been a friend of Che's. One day we went to have lunch at the famous bar, La Bodeguita del Medio—frequented by the likes of Hemingway and Nicolás Guillén—with Juan Martín Guevara (Patatín), the baby brother we had played with as teenagers. At one point in the conversation, the band began to play a song that went: Aquí se queda clara / la entrañable transparencia / de tu querida presencia / Comandante Che Guevara. *(Here it's plain to see / the true transparency / of your dear company / Commander Che Guevara).* It was a magical moment; I looked over at Juan Martín sitting there, so much like his

7 Pacho O'Donnell, *Che. La vida por un mundo mejor,* Buenos Aires, Sudamericana, 2003, p. 351.

brother, and I thought I saw Ernesto.

I left Cuba with a bittersweet feeling. I had seen the fruits of Ernesto's life up close: his children and the Revolution; but I also understood that I should have responded to my friend's call to join him. Today, I blame myself for not having taken part in that glorious revolutionary feat.

On my last trip to Cuba in April of 2005, I visited the Comandante Che Guevara Research Center, where his family is collecting all the mementos, documents and testimonials on the life of Ernesto. A few months later, I had the pleasure of welcoming and showing Camilo Guevara around all the places in Alta Gracia where his father and I had spent our childhood. All the information he gathered was to be added to the files at the Research Center in Cuba. I only hope that the stories I've told in this book also serve as a useful testimonial to shed even more light on the figure of Che.

In Cuba I met many others close to Ernesto who shared their memories of him with me: William Gálvez Rodríguez, a retired general who was second in command in the Camilo Cienfuegos column and who also does research and writes on Che; Freddy Ilunga, who, at thirteen, was Ernesto's French translator during his campaign in the Congo, today one of 31,000 African scholars working in Cuba. Such an easy-going, nice guy, Freddy made me laugh telling me of his first impressions of Ernesto.

"Who is this little white guy Fidel has sent us, always perfuming his mouth?" he'd say to his companions, until he learned that the "perfume" was really the medicine for Ernesto's asthma, which he had to use frequently in the jungle. I was also reunited with Ana María Erro, Ernesto's father's second wife, whom I had met in Buenos Aires before they moved to Cuba. She now lives with her children María Victoria, Ramiro and Ramón, named in honor of the *nom de guerre* used by his brother in Bolivia.

Ernesto's father passed away before I went to Cuba, but we had kept in touch until the very end. After the years I lived in Venezuela, back in Buenos Aires I resumed seeing the Guevara family with the same fondness as always. When my first son was born in 1973, we named him Ernesto after my friend. Through Ernesto's father, I was able to have him baptized by Father Carlos Mugica, later assassinated by the Triple A death squad (Argentine Anti-communist Alliance). It was a simple, poignant ceremony in the chapel of the neighborhood of Retiro. I remember that Mugica said that, for him, it was an honour to baptize the son of a friend of Che's.

In the following years, political persecution by the Triple A and the brutal Process of National Reorganization forced practically all of the Guevara family into exile. Those were dark, silent times when even communication by letter was dangerous. I've kept a letter sent to me by Ernesto's father from La Habana in 1982, in which he says: "I haven't written to you for obvious reasons, but I can assure you that I've kept you and your family in my thoughts always." That was when he let me know about the publication of his book on "Ernestito", published in Spain (he was referring to *Mi hijo el Che*). With Roberto Guevara, I maintain a friendship until this day. After his long exile, one day—democracy had already returned to Argentina—I ran into him on the street. He was at the corner of Viamonte and Paraná and suddenly, we saw each other. I couldn't believe it. As I hugged him, I said, "I thought I'd never see you again." We now get together when we can to reminisce and, of course, the main topic of our conversations is Ernesto.

I also continue to see another great friend from my

childhood, Carlos Figueroa. Ernesto left his mark on all of us in one way or another.

There were many other factors that pushed me toward the adventure of digging through my memory and writing this book: my conversations with Alberto Granado, who visits me every time he travels to Argentina; the moving film *Motorcycle Diaries*, which recounts Ernesto's and Alberto's first trip through Latin America; the publication in 2000 of Ernesto's diaries from our trip, which allowed me to relive all our adventures through his eyes; the creation of the museum in the Villa Nydia house in Alta Gracia, where the Guevara's had lived, that I contributed to with photographs and objects and that has become the meeting site for all of us who keep scraps of memory of Ernesto's life alive; and finally, because age doesn't come unaccompanied—at 76, even though I feel like a "spring chicken", I know I'm living on borrowed time and I can't put off what I now feel is my duty.

This book would not have been possible without the priceless collaboration of my now good friend Constanza Brunet, chief editor of Marea Editorial, who faithfully took down my memories as they came to me during our extended conversations together. I also appreciate the warmth and friendly family atmosphere that surrounded us as we worked: Daniel and their daughters Ana, Laura and Eugenia—who also patiently transcribed more than 20 hours of interviews—Rodi, Lole, Virginia and Katy, an affectionate and persistent cat who scratched me throughout our months together.

One sentence of Ernesto's revealed the true meaning of our wanderings through Latin America and how those trips of his youth marked his thinking and his commitment to the revolutionary struggle:

I was born in Argentina, that's no secret. I'm a Cuban

and an Argentine and—no offence to the illustrious sovereigns of Latin America—but I feel just as much a patriot of Latin America, of any Latin American country, and if it were necessary, I would be willing to give my life for the liberation of any of those countries, without requests, demands or exploitation of anyone.

Comprehending that he backed those words with his life in the Bolivian jungle was perhaps the final push I needed to get to the business of telling our story in those lands that he came to love as he hitchhiked or walked across them with nothing more than an empty stomach, tattered clothes and supreme enthusiasm.

Today as I write the final lines of this book, after having traveled again in my imagination and been reunited with my friend in uncountable memories, I feel that the same love and admiration I've always had for him have grown even more. In closing, I return to the words of writer Eduardo Galeano, who expressed much better than I can the thinking of all who admire Ernesto Guevara:

> Why is it that Che has that dangerous habit of rebirth? The more he's insulted, manipulated, betrayed, the more he comes to life. He has more lives than anyone. Might it not be that Che said what he thought and did what he said? Might that not be the reason he continues to be so extraordinary in a world where words and action very rarely come together and, when they do, they fail to greet each other because neither recognizes the other?[8]

Calica Ferrer,
Buenos Aires, September 2005

---

8 P. O'Donnell, Op. cit., p. 543.

My son Ernesto's baptism in the poor neighborhood of Retiro, August 1973. I had the honor of having him baptized by Father Carlos Mugica, assassinated by the Triple A shortly thereafter. He appears with us in the photo along with Ernesto Guevara senior, his wife Ana María Erro and little daughter María Victoria. The godparents were my brother Horacio Ferrer and Ana Inés Heller.

During my first trip to Cuba in 1990, I was reunited with Ana María Erro and her children María Victoria, already a teenager, and Ramón, named in honor of his brother's nom de guerre.

Here I am in Cuba with Hildita Guevara, Ernesto's eldest daughter, who has since passed away.

In the aquarium in La Habana with Celita Guevara, another of Ernesto's daughters, now a veterinarian.

With his
daughter Aleida
Guevara in
Almeijeidas
Hospital
in Cuba.

Ernesto's first grandchild, the
daughter of Aleida. Here she is
in the nursery school next to
Alberto Granado's house,
where I stayed during my first
visit to Cuba.

On the Isla de la Juventud with Alberto Granado, visiting the prison where the more than 1000 who participated in the Bay of Pigs invasion were held prisoner.

With Alberto Granado, visiting Colonia, Uruguay in 2004. Alberto had traveled to Argentina with his wife, Delia.

In the Ernesto "Che" Guevara Museum in Alta Gracia with two dear friends, Alberto Granado and Carlos Figueroa.

Here, Granado and I are in a place he never dreamed of visiting, the Pink House [Argentinean Presidential House]. For many years, Che Guevara was a taboo name for the dictatorial governments in Argentina. The administration of Néstor Kirchner invited us in 2004 on this official visit.

With Granado and Liborio Noval, a very important Cuban photographer who shared many hours of volunteer work with Ernesto. We were in the city of Santa Clara, Cuba, the site of the final battle of the victory of the Revolution. Behind us, the train that Che's column of men caused to de-rail.

This photo symbolizes a tribute to Ernesto because I'm with another great friend of his, Alberto Granado, standing in front of the mausoleum where he was laid to rest along with his comrades who fought and died with him in the Bolivian jungle. The photo was taken by Liborio Noval.

In the Comandante Che Guevara Research Center in La Habana during my last trip to Cuba in 2005; I'm with Granado and one of Ernesto's grandchildren, the daughter of Camilo Guevara.

In the Cuban-African Friendship House, I met Freddy Ilunga, today a neurosurgeon, who at 13 had been Che's French interpreter during his African campaign. The director of that institution is Albertico Granado, my dear nephew.

With Camilo Guevara March beside what was left of the swimming pool at that grand Hotel Sierras. We are sitting on the same bench where his father and I were photographed hugging each other when we were 15.

"Calica, Ernesto says if you want, the doors are wide open to you, but that you should know that soon Cuba will declare itself a socialist republic and break all ties with the capitalist world," Alberto told me when he returned from a trip to Cuba. And he gave me this frogskin wallet that Ernesto had sent me as a gift. I didn't go.

In May 2005, Camilo Guevara came to visit Argentina to collect information about his father's life here. I had the honor of being his official guide in Alta Gracia. Here we are seated on the stairs of what was my childhood home. His father and I had posed there together at every family birthday party.

On that same trip, Camilo and I visited the Ernesto Che Guevara Museum housed in Villa Nydia, one of the houses his family had rented in Alta Gracia.

TABLE OF CONTENTS

This edition of *Becoming Che*
was printed in Nuevo Offset,
Viel 1444, Buenos Aires,
October 2006